WILLIAM C. WILSON
the Fifth General Superintendent

WILLIAM C. WILSON
the Fifth General Superintendent

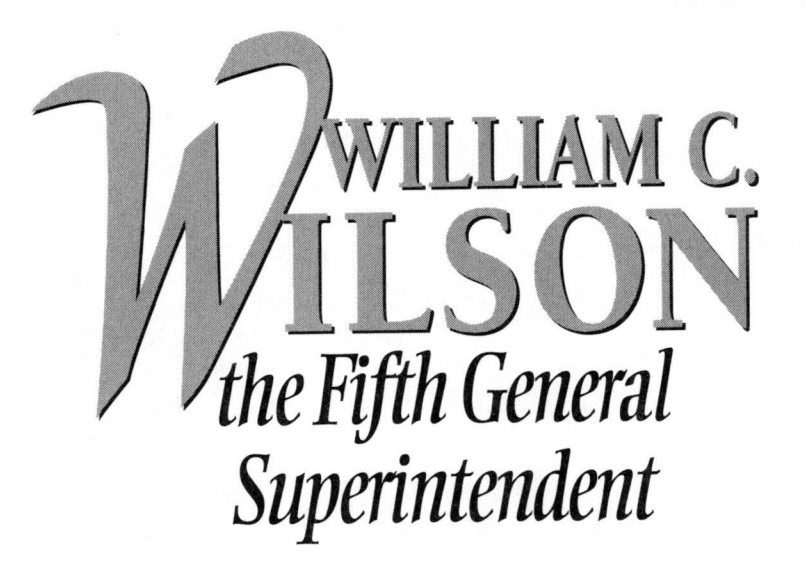

MALLALIEU WILSON

Nazarene Publishing House
Kansas City, Missouri

Copyright 1995
by Nazarene Publishing House

ISBN 083-411-5573

Printed in the
United States of America

Cover Design: Crandall Vail and Mike Walsh

10 9 8 7 6 5 4 3 2 1

Contents

Foreword   7

1. William Columbus Wilson   11
2. Lum Grows Up   17
3. A New Crisis Experience   21
4. From Plow to Pulpit   27
5. Circuit Rider   31
6. The Evangelist   35
7. Miss Sarah   39
8. The Holiness Revival in Kentucky   43
9. A New Church Home   49
10. The Church Grows   57
11. Pasadena   61
12. The Family Matures   69
13. Influencing a Young Denomination   75
14. Colleagues   81
15. The Highest Office   87

Foreword

William C. Wilson bridged many of the contradictions within the early Church of the Nazarene. He bridged its underlying regionalism, knowing well the sectional attitudes of his native South, while growing to appreciate the ethos of early 20th-century California. Likewise, he bridged the early denomination's divided mind over ethics, understanding (and for a time preaching) an ethic of legalism but gradually accepting the view that holiness provides liberty, not law, in the Christian life.

Wilson preached the reality of crisis experiences of grace, yet he acknowledged that *his* call to preach was a gradual awareness, not some distinct "voice of God" to which associates sometimes testified. He was pressed into administration by an infant denomination, though he loved to preach and helped awaken a preaching vocation in three of his children. Finally, when W. C. Wilson could least afford the financial sacrifice of being general superintendent, he was elected to that office.

Wilson faced the ironies of his life with exceedingly great grace. He was, above all, a preacher of reconciliation, first between sinners and Divine Grace; second, among and between those who confess together their loyalty to Christ and His Church.

Wilson's ministry was assisted by wives and children who knew personally the grace he preached. His older children experienced the grief of their young mother's death, the breakup of their home, and the family's resurrection after Wilson's remarriage. Together the Wilson family experienced the helplessness of an infant's death and the tragic loss of a grown child shortly after her marriage. But they also experienced joyous reunions, enjoyed some "good pastorates," and found time in

California to spend some happy moments together on the beach.

Only Mallalieu Wilson could have written this intimate portrait of his father, W. C. Wilson. Mallalieu knew personally many of the founders of the Church of the Nazarene and can be characterized as one of its "founding youths." Born in 1898, he participated in the church's early life on the West Coast and in its pioneer youth programs. He grew up around Phineas Bresee, John Goodwin, Edward F. Walker, A. O. Hendricks, E. P. Ellyson, Seth Rees, and others who led the church in southern California and beyond. He knew them through church, camp meeting, district assembly, and through the intimate community of Pasadena and its Nazarene University (later Pasadena College), where he was a student leader in both the academy (high school) and the college.

This account reflects Mallalieu Wilson's insight into personalities who shaped the Church of the Nazarene in its formative years. Behind his views there are sometimes the opinions of his father. But the book also illuminates people and issues significant in the broader Holiness Movement.

Above all, it records the story of William C. Wilson, whose journey of faith led him across the landscape of scattered Holiness sects into the Church of the Nazarene and from one end of the nation to the other. In the providence of God, Wilson was elected by peers and laity to be one of their general superintendents.

STAN INGERSOL
Nazarene Archives
Kansas City

THE FAMILY

William Columbus Wilson, 1866-1915
First wife: Eliza Jones, 1867-93
CHILDREN:
Guy LaFayette Wilson, 1887-1968
Bertha Wilson Lillenas, 1889-1945
Hallie Wilson Franklin, 1891-1912
Ruth Wilson Orrin, 1893-1954

◊

Second wife: Sarah Ragsdale, 1873-1955
CHILDREN:
Mallalieu Archie Wilson, 1898—
Fitzgerald Wilson, B. AND D. 1899
Deborah Wilson Grobe, 1901—
William Willard Wilson, 1904-73
Jeanette Wilson Runquist, 1906-61

1

WILLIAM COLUMBUS WILSON

Headlines from the *Los Angeles Times,*
Monday, December 20, 1915:

Strange Coincidence
WORK, DIE, AND REST TOGETHER
Pentecostal Nazarene Church
Loses Second Leader

Rev. W. C. Wilson
Follows Dr. Bresee to Grave

Both Elected to Same High Office
at Kansas City

Phineas F. Bresee—"Dr. Bresee" to his colleagues and parishioners in Methodist and Nazarene circles—is well known in Wesleyan-Holiness circles as the late-19th-century founder of the Church of the Nazarene in Los Angeles. This was one of three groups that united to form the Pentecostal Church of the Nazarene, and in the united denomination he was the outstanding early leader.

General Superintendent W. C. Wilson is less well known. Wilson was much younger than Dr. Bresee but was actively associated with the older preacher for the last 12 years of their lives. He played a unique part in the early life of the new denomination, both in the Western parent body and in the united church.

When Wilson went to California in 1905, the Church of the Nazarene was expanding. In the following years he helped establish three of the largest and strongest congregations in the church: Long Beach, Upland, and Pasadena First. He served on the first committee of the California church that worked out a basis of union with the Association of Pentecostal Churches of America, a group centered in the Northeast—a union consummated at Chicago in 1907, creating the Pentecostal Church of the Nazarene. He was acquainted with leaders of the Southern-based Holiness Church of Christ, whose union with the Pentecostal Nazarenes in 1908 was recognized 15 years later as the anniversary date of the present denomination. W. C. Wilson was also well acquainted with Rev. J. O. McClurkan, founder of the Pentecostal Mission in Nashville—a relatively short distance from Wilson's Kentucky home. The churches growing out of the Pentecostal Mission also became part of the Pentecostal Church of the Nazarene in 1915.

Wilson was also involved in the creation of Nazarene University, now Point Loma Nazarene College. While he pastored in Upland, California, one of his church members gave the gift that established the school's first campus. Later, as pastor of Pasadena First Church, Wilson inspected the 134-acre Hugus Ranch and was involved in the college's relocation there. He taught in the college for a time and later spent his time unsparingly as a trustee, sharing with Dr. Bresee and others the burdens of the school.

As superintendent of the Southern California District, which included the state of Arizona, Wilson often conferred with Bresee. Although they shared similar views from the beginning of their relationship, Wilson's value of Bresee's insight increased with each year of their association. As the older man's strength declined, Wilson assumed more and more of his responsibilities—even traveling in Eastern states to hold Dr. Bresee's district assemblies. In 1915 Wilson was elected to the general superintendency and immediately began holding assemblies while his colleague returned to Los Angeles to die. Before his first slate of assemblies was quite completed, he returned to Pasadena and shortly followed his beloved leader to the other world.

What were W. C. Wilson's origins? What background did this young man have who rose to such positions of influence in the last decade of his short life? Perhaps we should begin with glimpses of the two men, Bresee and Wilson, 20 years before they met for the first time.

The year: 1886. The place: Pasadena, California.

Two wagons pulled by teams of heavy draft horses moved slowly up the dusty road known later as Orange Grove Avenue. Near the present-day reviewing stand for the Tournament of Roses New Year's Day Parade, they turned east and went down the hill on Colorado Street to their destination— the Methodist Episcopal church and parsonage. The wagons were carrying the furniture of the new pastor, Rev. Phineas F. Bresee.

Pasadena had been a sheep ranch only a few years before. It was divided into 40-acre tracts, with some planted in orchards of seedling oranges, lemons, apricots, and other fruits. When the boom of the early 1880s hit southern California, a group of small buildings at Colorado Street and Fair Oaks Avenue began to expand rapidly. A few blocks east of this, a group of Methodists had started a new building at the site where the First United Methodist Church stands now, over a century later.

Under the leadership of Pastor Bresee, this little church had a most spectacular growth in the next few years. Bresee became a district superintendent and the most outstanding Methodist preacher in southern California. He was a trustee for the University of Southern California and, for a time, acting chairman of the Board of Trustees. However, when he asked to be stationed at a non-Methodist mission in the slums of Los Angeles, his bishop refused to give his approval. Bresee worked for the mission anyway, and after one year of this type of work, he and many of his associates felt the need for an organized church to meet their needs and those of their families. With J. P. Widney, a prominent physician and former president of the University of Southern California, Bresee started an independent church in Los Angeles that expanded and became part of an international denomination that now carries the name originally chosen for that one congregation in Los Angeles: Church of the Nazarene.

The year: 1886. The place: Hopkins County, Kentucky.

In a farm home two teenagers were being married by a Baptist minister. The boy was William Columbus (Lum) Wilson. The young groom had acquired a farm and a home. His bride was a serious girl and used to hard work. Both were devout Christians, and Bible reading and prayer were observed daily in their home from the start.

Lum Wilson had little in his ancestry, environment, education, or early life to suggest he might ever become a religious leader. The *Los Angeles Times* reporter, in writing of his death, stated that he came from "an old Southern family of ministers, physicians, and lawyers." This was as fanciful and as far from fact as the statement in the same article that he and Dr. Bresee were buried in the same cemetery.

There were other preachers in Lum's family, but most came after him, not before him. He tried to trace his family tree but was unable to go back more than four or five generations to a 12-year-old boy who ran away from his widowed mother in England and came to the New World to start his branch of the Wilson family. Little is known of that ancestor except that he settled in Virginia and that he or his son moved to Kentucky around 1800.

Lum's grandfather fought in the War of 1812 and was captured by Indians, who forced him to run the gauntlet several times. He so impressed his captors with his bravery that they wanted to adopt him. He was given the alternative of being tomahawked—so to avoid certain death, he agreed to the adoption. Before the war ended, he was exchanged for an Indian prisoner and reunited with his own people. His descendants seemed to inherit his trait of extreme bravery.

Lum's father was a Civil War officer, Capt. J. C. Wilson of the Kentucky Cavalry. Southern sentiment was strong in that section of Kentucky, but J. C. Wilson was so firmly pro-Union in convictions that he was kidnapped by Southern sympathizers and taken from his farm and family. After he was rescued by local Union militiamen, he organized and led a company that was accepted into the Union army. He was commended for bravery in helping stop Confederate Gen. John Hunt Morgan's attempt to cut through Kentucky and raid Union territory north of the Ohio River.

Although Captain Wilson made no profession of religion until Lum was older, he was an upright, moral man. He totally abstained from alcohol, which was unusual for that time and area. The captain's father, the Indian fighter, was such a heavy drinker that he lost most of his wealth. As a young teenager, J. C. Wilson told his father, "If I ever see you drunk in front of the family again, I'll leave home and never return." The threat was carried out the next time the poor old man staggered in.

Lum's knowledge of his maternal ancestry was even more abbreviated and inaccurate. His mother was Eliza Jane Majors, daughter of Helen and Alexander Majors. Although a Kentuckian with the same name as Grandfather Majors founded the Pony Express, no relationship with him has been traced. From his mother's side of the family, Lum Wilson was related to seafaring men and pioneers.

2

LUM GROWS UP

Lum was born December 22, 1866, in a log cabin in Hopkins County, Kentucky, near the small town of Manitou. A year later his father bought a farm 10 miles north, where Lum grew up.

Schools were held only a few months each winter, and Lum seemed more interested in rabbit hunting than in reading. There were no frills to his education. Only bare fundamentals were taught. He never needed much arithmetic, and what he failed to learn about reading was made up in later life. There was little to read in the home of a poor tobacco farmer anyway. He did, however, read all his father's military books. His schooling completely failed at teaching him one skill in particular—he never could spell, except phonetically.

Church advantages were no better than educational ones. There were not many churches, and few had full-time pastors or regular services every Sunday. Lum's mother was converted at 13, and she read the Bible regularly, especially on Sundays. Preachers were entertained in their home as they traveled their circuits or came to hold meetings.

These revival meetings greatly impressed Lum. He trembled under the vivid preaching of hellfire and Judgment Day, but his parents believed in adult baptism, not in childhood conversion. No one invited him to become a Christian, so he suffered his nightmares in loneliness.

During this time Lum made an unusual scientific observation. He noted that in winter the shadows lengthened, and in spring they shortened. He marked this change by notching a log in the barn to indicate the changed length of a gatepost shadow. Each year as the winter solstice approached, he lived in anxiety that the noonday shadow might pass the mark he had made the previous December. He feared that if this happened, the world would end. When the shadow began to retreat each year for several consecutive years, he became convinced of the stability of nature, and his fears subsided—and along with them his worries about sin.

Lum probably felt condemned most for his temper tantrums. He was sickly for a few years as a small boy and felt later that his parents spoiled him. His mother said that he had always been a good boy, obedient to his parents; Captain Wilson would not have tolerated anything else.

He became more mischievous in adolescence but used no lurid confessions from his past in later evangelistic preaching. One Sunday night, though, when he went as usual to the little Missionary Baptist church where his parents were members, he slipped out with several other boys during the first song and went raccoon hunting. They were so successful that when the congregation was dismissed and began filing out, the boys had already caught, killed, and skinned the coon and were roasting it over a fire they had built in the corner of the churchyard.

Even in his preconversion boyhood years, Lum always prayed a great deal. Thus, when a Methodist preacher named Rev. John Keen spoke to him kindly and said he had been praying for the boy, Lum accepted the invitation to go to an altar and was definitely converted. This was in the Providence Methodist Church, where his grandmother, Helen Majors, had recently been buried in the churchyard. Although the church where Lum's parents were members broadly applied Paul's injunctions against women speaking in church, Eliza Jane forgot that when she saw her 16-year-old boy seeking God at last. Rushing to his side, she dropped on her knees and began praying loudly and earnestly. Lum felt clearly saved. His peace was sweet, and he was very happy. The next morning, he took his cherished fiddle and smashed it against the backyard fence. Years later, he regretted the action and ascribed it to a mistaken religious prejudice.

Lum began leading public prayer and doing personal work to win others, but in less than a year he grew cold and ceased to make any effort to serve God. It did not take long to become sick of sin, however; and when he was reclaimed, it was with a firm determination to be true as long as he lived.

In 1886 Lum married Eliza Jones, who had celebrated her 19th birthday less than two weeks before the wedding. Lum had bought a farm, and they moved into their own home.

Eliza was the daughter of Gaston Jones, an ex-Confederate soldier. All four of his daughters were large, handsome women with strong characters, but Eliza was shorter than her tall sisters. She was a member of the Missionary Baptist church, like her parents and Lum's. Lum now joined the same church.

The Missionary Baptists were so named because they supported church work, such as missions and Sunday Schools, that hard-shell Baptists opposed. Like their hard-shell brethren, though, Missionary Baptists practiced closed Communion, allowing only those who had been immersed and received into the local church to participate in the Lord's Supper. Like Lum, his three brothers later withdrew from the Missionary Baptists, though none of them followed him into the Church of the Nazarene.

Lum and Eliza were not merely nominal church members. They read the Bible and prayed together each evening, taking turns leading the devotional time. Both were somewhat timid about it. In all other things Lum did not know the meaning of fear, but when visitors were present, he always was relieved if it was Eliza's turn to read and pray.

Churches were not very numerous, especially in rural areas. In many communities there were no regular preaching services. Even where a church had been erected, there might be a sermon only once or twice a month. One pastor might have as many as 8 or 10 congregations to care for. Lum began to feel that they should have public worship in their home on Sunday mornings. To this Eliza gladly agreed, so they inaugurated such services and held them whenever they would not interfere with the meetings in their own church or with special meetings in a nearby church. Frequently they felt "graciously blessed" in these services, and at such times Lum sometimes felt that he might someday have to preach. These feelings were rather vague and did not persist. Meanwhile, Lum and Eliza became the parents of a boy, Guy LaFayette.

3

A NEW CRISIS EXPERIENCE

At 22 Lum had his own farm, wife, and son and was content to live in the rural community where he had grown up. But somehow this bashful young farm boy entered upon a new calling. In spite of insufficient schooling, he became a successful preacher, played a great part in establishing the Church of the Nazarene and the school that is now Point Loma Nazarene College, and was elected to the highest office in his church.

It may seem incredible that Lum had never heard of the experience that John Wesley preached as "Christian perfection," "the second blessing," or "the great salvation." The subject had been neglected by Methodists in trying to convert the rough frontiersmen in America, and although revived about the middle of the century in the "Higher Life" movement, it was rarely preached among Southern Methodists.

Here is Lum's story of this crisis experience in his life:

> In the spring of 1889, an evangelist by the name of Charles Royster came to our hometown, Hanson, Kentucky, and commenced a meeting in the Methodist Episcopal church, South. I was notified of the meeting and invited to attend. On going out to the service, I learned that the pastor was not in sympathy with the preaching of the evangelist and had merely let him have the use of his house. The pastor was present but took no part.
>
> My first impression of the preacher and his work was that he was young and had more zeal than knowledge. A little later I determined from my standpoint

that he had been backslidden and had gotten reclaimed and concluded that he was sanctified. I thought I would quit the meeting and take my rest as I was busy, it being May and I was farming. But the Sabbath came, and I knew the pastor was to preach; so I went over to hear him settle things, for I had heard that would take place. The pastor was there in great shape.

He opened fire on the sanctified folks and the "second blessings," as he called them. He said he believed in a hundred blessings, and a good many of us thought that what he said was timely and well said. But the thing that seemed a little strange to me was that the evangelist did not seem offended in the least and at many things said "Amen."

At the evening service there was a large crowd. I was in my seat to hear the pastor finish the second blessings. He said many hard things about the people that were sowing contention and causing so much discord in the land. He said, "If you will look close after this is over, in place of the hoofprints, in my opinion, you will find the claws."

I felt like the young evangelist would take the first train out of town, but I was surprised. At the close of the sermon the pastor said, "I suppose you will close your meeting?"

The evangelist answered in a very pleasant way. "No, brother, not if we can have use of your church."

The pastor replied, "That will be with the trustees. I will not be responsible for the meeting."

One of the trustees, a tobacco buyer, said, "I have the key, and this house will be locked."

The pastor seemed composed. There was some whispering around, and some of us felt that the pastor was the right man in the right place, and that the trouble was all over.

As there had been scarcely any fruit from the first week of meetings and the pastor was unwilling to be responsible for the meeting, we all thought that would end the thing. But the evangelist did not leave town. The next day it was reported that he would try to get another church. The Methodists talked it over and concluded it would not be wise to lock out one of their own preachers and have someone else let him in, and so that evening the bell rang out clear, inviting us to come again and hear the evangelist. I went over that evening to hear him skin the pastor. There was a good crowd out.

The preacher said, "The Methodists have kindly given us the use of the house to continue services in, and the meeting will go right on."

He took a text and preached. He seemed very happy. He preached sanctification like we all believed it, and he never referred to any of the hard things the pastor had said. Somewhere along about that time I began to think that possibly the brother had something the pastor did not have, and so I began to listen a little closer.

My wife became much interested in the meeting. As we began to search the Bible more closely, somehow I became very serious about the matter. There seemed to be a heart hunger spring up in my very being, although I said but little. I prayed much. A few days passed by, and at an evening service the preacher said, "At the close of my sermon, we will have a praise meeting."

Wife was one of the first to talk. She said, "I am conscious that I am converted and love God, but somehow I am convinced that some of you people have freedom that I do not, and I want to be remembered in prayer."

She took her seat. Others told how God had revealed their need of holiness to them, how hungry they became, and how He satisfied them when they were sanctified wholly. Somehow, I felt a little blue.

Wife rose again and said, "I want you to pray for me that God will give me liberty. I am not sure as to what I need. I do not say I want to be sanctified. I don't know now that I understand that, but I must have victory and liberty. I try to do my duty, but I have a man-fearing spirit about me, and I must have freedom. And I believe it is God's will I should. So you remember me when you pray."

She sat down. I felt uneasy. It began to look as though wife would go to seek a second blessing. I had a real struggle to keep from talking to her in reference to the matter.

When we reached home that night and entered the house, I lit a lamp, and she walked across to the lounge and, kneeling, began to cry aloud and said, "You pray for me. My heart is not clean."

I do not remember all I said, but I prayed as best I could, but I felt cold and scared. The thought came to me that she had never been converted. I said, "Well, if she was never converted, what about my case? I am sure she is as pious as me."

I finished my prayer, and she cried louder, "God, give me a clean heart." I left the room, went out on the porch, and listened, thinking that I might hear someone coming by that way who understood how to pray for and talk to persons in that condition, for I was sure I never saw anyone in that fix. By this time she had fallen over on the floor. I tried to get her to get up and get on the bed.

She said, "Let me alone. I must have a clean heart. I can't stand this."

I said, "You trust God. He alone can help you."

About this time our little boy began to cry, rousing from his nap. I took him up in my arms and felt some more at home trying to quiet him than trying to tell my wife how to get that which I knew nothing of myself.

But in a few minutes there came a pleasant smile over her face, and she said, "Praise God! I've gotten the victory."

She rose to her feet and, walking the floor, shouted for some time. Guy seemed all right—since Mamma looked so pleasant. I felt better, and I began to sing:

> *On Jordan's stormy banks I stand,*
> *And cast a wistful eye*
> *To Canaan's fair and happy land,*
> *Where my possessions lie.*
> —SAMUEL STENNETT

The song was more appropriate than I thought—for at that time the good Lord blessed me with a big blessing, and I shouted all over the house, jumped, and made a great deal of noise. But in a few minutes I stopped, sat down, and it seemed to me as though something said to me, "You have cut a big swell."

I said, "Yes, that is so."

"What if your neighbors should come in to see what is the matter? What would you tell them?"

About this time I began to feel bad. I noticed wife continued to wave her hands and say, "I am so free!"

The Lord showed me there and then that I only had dashes of glory and not a constant shining forth to glory. In a few days I was seeking the blessing in good earnest in every way except God's way. I did not want to go to the altar, but bye the bye I said, "Yes, I will go!"

It was a struggle. The pastor happened to come in and sat down at my side while the preacher was preaching. I've never been sure who sent him. At any rate, he looked twice as large as usual to me that afternoon, but when the sermon was over and the altar was presented, I said yes to God and knelt at the altar. I was so melted it seemed I could not say one word. And suddenly my strength seemed to give way, and I fell over on the floor. The pastor sitting by my side left the room, and I heard him say as he stepped over my feet, "There is no need of that."

I have always felt sure if he could have seen the invisible Hand that was separating carnality from my heart, he would not have spoken so rashly in the presence of the Heavenly Friend.

I lay on the floor some time. I seemed weak; but as my strength came, there seemed to be a sacredness about the hour that I can't explain. I only wanted to be alone. There was an emptiness about my heart that I had never felt—a sweetness in the thought that I was forever the Lord's that I can't explain. I did not shout nor care to talk, but there was rest in the true sense, peace, deep and sweet.

As I started from the church, after walking about one square, I met a colored man. I told him what had happened. He grinned. It seemed all heaven smiled on me. And at once the tides of divine life began to rise in my soul. By the time I reached home a quarter of a mile away, I was shouting aloud.

That was on the 14th of May, 1889, and it has been settled ever since.*

---

*W. C. Wilson, unpublished MS, "Sketch of My Life and Travels," dated 1905. In the William C. Wilson Collection, Nazarene Archives, Kansas City, Missouri.

4

FROM PLOW TO PULPIT

In the 19th century the majority of preachers probably came from farm families, for more children were born on farms than in cities. It may have been too that the ministry offered the most open door to a career off the farm and away from the hardships of rural life. There could have been some like the young man in the well-worn story who saw the letters "GPC" emblazoned in the sky and concluded that they meant "Go preach Christ," when other people felt they should have been more correctly interpreted "Go plow corn."

Lum never had a vision in which he was called to preach. In fact, he admitted that he could never point to a definite time when he received a "call." From the beginning of his Christian life he felt at times that possibly he might preach someday, but at other times he thought it "just a whim of the brain." Unlike many preachers, he was not rebellious against giving his life to the ministry, but on the contrary he feared that his desire to preach might lead him to choose the ministry when the Lord did not want it so.

It used to seem that every preacher who told his experience of receiving the second blessing had as the final crucial test of his consecration the question "Will you preach?" The corollary was the implication that every boy who was consecrated to God and received the second blessing was expected to be a preacher. In like case, a girl must be willing to marry a preacher or become a foreign missionary.

Although the question of preaching did not enter Lum's

mind in seeking the experience of entire sanctification, the experience itself very positively led him to enter the ministry. The wonderful grace that had come to his heart was so great that within a few weeks the desire to share this truth with others obsessed him day and night.

Lum realized that he lacked education and that none of his relatives were preachers, but he was so happy in his newfound grace that he soon decided he would try to preach and continue until he made an utter failure or success. When he had fully settled it in his mind to make this trial, he sent word to his old neighborhood, where he had grown up, that he would preach at the Methodist Episcopal church on the coming Sunday if there were no objections. The announcement was made, and when the time arrived he was astonished that a large crowd of neighbors, friends, and foes were present. All seemed full of curiosity.

He opened the service with song and prayer and took as his text the "biggest text in the Bible"—1 Thess. 5:23: "And the very God of peace sanctify you wholly; and I pray God your whole spirit and soul and body be preserved blameless unto the coming of our Lord Jesus Christ."

In writing about this later, Lum said, "The Lord helped me in a very gracious way and blessed me until it seemed that my heart could not have had more rest if I had been inside the jasper walls. That night I slept as sweet as a child, and from that day to this—which has been 20 years—there has never been a shadow of doubt in reference to my divine call to the ministry."

He proved that he believed he was called to preach by immediately going into churches, schoolhouses, or even private homes when occasions permitted. He witnessed to full salvation wherever he went, and people were saved and sanctified in the meetings he conducted. This confirmed his belief in his call.

Things were not all rosy, however. There was much opposition to preaching the possibility of having a higher state of grace than people had known about before. He was shocked that church and friends who he thought would help instead tried to hinder his work—or so it seemed to him. The cold reception given him and Eliza when they testified to having received the grace of entire sanctification led them to withdraw from the Baptist fellowship and join the Methodist Episcopal Church, which at least historically accepted this doctrine. This was the largest branch of American Methodism and was predominantly Northern. From it the Methodist Episcopal Church, South, had broken off in 1844 over the slavery issue.

A transforming religious experience often prompts a real desire to learn. So it was with Lum. After he had preached about a year, he disposed of the farm and took his family, now including a second child, to a school at Bremen, Kentucky. At 24, Lum studied the elementary subjects left off years before. In three or four months he satisfactorily completed the last 4 years of elementary school with one exception—spelling. But at least he could read it himself, and until later years he had no occasion to write for other people. When he did later write for publication and in official church correspondence, his phonetic spelling was based on the way words were pronounced with a Kentucky accent. This was often puzzling to others.

Many religious colleges in the 19th century were begun by devout souls with no concept of the costs or methods of administering such schools. Sometimes the trustees found a capable, experienced, educated preacher with enlightened concepts of school governance. More often, they settled for a mediocre person who ruled with an iron hand. One problem for Lum was the regulation that no student leave town without the express permission of the president. Lum had already accepted nearby preaching appointments on Sunday, and the college president severely reprimanded him. Lum was as apologetic as his independent nature allowed, but he made it clear he would preach whenever there was an opportunity.

One such opportunity was at the college's community church, where Lum and a senior student were elected to serve as regular preachers. This was a blow to the school's president, who had hoped to be elected himself. Lum soon excused himself from the task and asked the president to preach in his place. The president was not received as well and eventually resigned from the college.

The trustees took a referendum of the students to determine their choice of closing the school or continuing with a senior student as acting president. The students voted overwhelmingly to continue, but the trustees decided to close the school. Lum's formal education ended.

5

CIRCUIT RIDER

After his school closed, Lum Wilson held meetings in various parts of Kentucky during the summer. In September he was appointed to the Greenville Circuit, a part of the Louisville District of the Methodist Episcopal Church. The district was under Presiding Elder Rev. E. L. Shepard, a sanctified minister. The circuit had three small churches, with a total annual remuneration of $180. He entered the work with much joy. Eliza's attitude was a great help, for she was willing to make sacrifices and was radiantly happy in her experience of full salvation. She delighted in telling the Good News to others.

The Methodist preachers who had charge of a string of churches were called "circuit riders," but Lum did not own a horse, so for more than a year he was a circuit "walker." Nevertheless, he held special meetings at each of his three churches. There were "a good number of conversions, a few sanctified, and a fair number of additions." He also held meetings in a schoolhouse and organized a new congregation there. Two boys, one converted and the other sanctified under Lum's ministry, felt called to preach. With his encouragement they entered the ministry and became successful pastors.

Lum was appointed to the Vine Grove Circuit the following year. This circuit had eight churches, all poor and small, scattered over a large area. Lum still had no horse for part of the year, but he preached regularly at all eight appointments, visited people in their homes, and held special "protracted meetings" in all the appointed preaching places. Many were converted or sanctified. One member on the circuit was a young woman who later became nationally known as "Aunt Betty Whitehead," author of a column in the *Pentecostal Herald,* the leading Holiness paper in the South. She often expressed appreciation for Lum's ministry during the year he pastored the Vine Grove Circuit. She later married the great Henry Clay Morrison, a dominant personality in the Southern Holiness Movement.

Not all members were appreciative of Lum's services. He organized a Holiness prayer meeting on Friday nights for those in one church who professed the second blessing of entire sanctification. A church trustee, greatly displeased, went to the church, nailed two of the doors shut, and locked the third door. He then sent his children to the nearby public school to have the teacher announce that the prayer meeting would be held Sunday night instead of Friday night. He asked Lum to support him in this action, but Lum refused, and the trustee declared that holiness would ruin the church. After giving the pastor some further advice, he mentioned that he paid more into the church than anyone else and stated that he would not collect or pay one cent on Lum's salary. With that he threw down his key to the church and walked off in a huff.

Lum wrote later that God kept him in perfect peace through this. He went to see the trustee again, who admitted wrong but still opposed the preaching of holiness. Lum's reply was, "Brother, I respect you as a man, but I must obey God. He sanctified me and called me to the ministry. I must be true, even if I never get one cent from you or this church."

This unpleasant experience did not change his relationship with the man or his family, and in time the man returned to the church and even seemed to respect Lum for his stand. The church paid the pastor's salary in full that year, and from all eight Vine Grove churches Lum received $260 for the year's work.

The year at Vine Grove held other difficult experiences as well. The change from muscular outdoor work to the stress-inducing pressures of ministry affected Lum's health. While some experiences naturally create inner turmoil, there were some beliefs among early Holiness people that were also harmful to their bodies, such as the idea that medicines were sinful. Lum does not appear to have subscribed to this idea, however.

Before he had a horse, Lum walked from a Sunday morning appointment to his afternoon appointment, although he could have ridden a train. Plunging out of the steamy church, dripping with perspiration, he plowed through several miles in a bitter snowstorm, took pneumonia, and almost died. In bed he pondered the wisdom of the Holiness Movement's blanket prohibitions, such as that against riding trains on Sunday. He also considered other viewpoints, such as premillennialism, that he had acquired from older Holiness preachers. He decided to study these further and limit his preaching to doctrines more clearly taught in the Bible. All this had a profound influence in shaping his thinking and preaching and prepared him to join so wholeheartedly with P. F. Bresee in the Church of the Nazarene a few years later.

Tragedy struck at the close of the conference year in 1893. Lum went to the annual conference in Louisville to make his report, while Eliza visited her father's home in Hanson. She arrived on Saturday and by Sunday was sick with typhoid fever. Lum hastened to her side. The following Saturday she asked Lum to read the Bible and pray with her and then to call in the children, four of them now: Guy, Bertha, Hallie, and Ruth (who was only four months old). Eliza talked to all present, telling how happy she was and asking them to meet her in heaven. She embraced each child and seemed to pray silently for them. Then with a faint whisper, "Bless God," she was gone.

Eliza had talked to Lum about what she thought he should arrange for the children, asked him to be true to holiness, and requested that on the rock at her grave there be only her name, the dates, and Heb. 12:14: "Follow peace with all men, and holiness, without which no man shall see the Lord."

6

THE EVANGELIST

After Eliza's death, Lum was unable to go on with pastoral work. His four children were placed with relatives, and he preached as an evangelist until he remarried a couple of years later.

It was rare in those days for preachers to spend all their time holding revivals. In some of the early Holiness writings, there are violent denunciations of pastors who called an outside preacher to hold a revival for them. If a man claimed to be sanctified, he was supposed to have the baptism of the Holy Ghost and was expected to have revivals under his own preaching.

In the early days almost all Methodist pastors were more like evangelists than like pastors in the conventional sense. A circuit rider would be kept busy most of the first year holding one special meeting after another in his charge. There would be no second year, for the Methodist concept of "itinerancy" (or traveling ministry) required that preachers move annually. As Methodists lengthened the permissable term of pastoral service and more pulpits were filled with men talented in administration, visitation, and a teaching type of preaching, such men would call on other pastors more gifted in evangelistic preaching to help in the annual protracted meeting. With a shortage of evangelistic pastors available for loan, some pastors forsook the annual revival meeting—or called on someone who specialized as a revivalist.

For Holiness preachers, this was a golden opportunity to preach their doctrine to congregations who had never heard it preached except in the vaguest terms. It was not altogether unusual for the pastor to join many of his most spiritual members at the altar. All Methodist preachers were required to testify that they had received this blessing of perfection in love before they could be admitted to the ministry, or else to state that they were "groaning after it."

The antiperfectionist bishops were glad to encourage Holiness preachers to enter the field of evangelism, as it spared them the embarrassment of having to appoint them to churches that were trying to avoid such pastors. Evangelists expected no guarantee that they would be kept busy or that their remuneration would be sufficient to cover traveling expenses for long distances between meetings.

Lum extended his range of travel as he became better known. His meetings were held generally in Kentucky or nearby states. In his early days as an evangelist, he often held meetings without an invitation from any church or individual. He especially enjoyed preaching in the Cumberland Mountains of Kentucky and Tennessee and in the Ozarks of Arkansas and Missouri. Those people were isolated, neglected, and almost unknown to the rest of the United States. Moreover, the lowland parts of these states were not strongly churched areas.

When Lum planned to enter a community uninvited, he sought a centrally located town, often the county seat. Sometimes he secured permission to use a schoolhouse, but he preferred an opera house or a courthouse auditorium. When a preaching place was arranged, he would borrow a wooden soapbox, set it in the street, and preach briefly from it, announcing the time and place of the first service. A crowd gathered easily, and once Lum spoke, they returned, bringing others with them.

After the sermon he might go out to the nearest creek for a drink of branch water and try to satisfy his hunger with wild blackberries. His night's rest might be on a bench in the place where he had preached. His next day's room and board might be the same, and this could continue for days until someone invited him home for a more comfortable bed and a more varied diet.

Nearly always there were scores of conversions in the meetings. Converts sometimes numbered in the hundreds. When the harvest of sinners had been well threshed, Lum would preach second-blessing holiness, and some always sought this experience.

The roughness of some communities where Lum preached was appalling. At one brush arbor camp meeting, unconverted men and boys amused themselves by circling the congregation during the sermons and firing guns over the heads of the people. Leaves and twigs would flutter down as bullets cut them loose. Lum preached on and noticed that even the hard-faced women never batted an eye but gave him their undivided attention.

In another community, a local bully who ran off earlier preachers boasted that he would horsewhip Lum and run him out. Lum let it be known that he was not afraid and that the boaster was welcome to try. He was one of the more peaceful of the rural Holiness preachers, but he was too much like his father and grandfather to let any "Philistine" defy the army of the Lord and get away with it.

The revivalism of the day was often characterized by strong emotional tides that were expressed physically, sometimes without inhibitions. Lum was personally free in expressing his religious feelings audibly and physically, and he believed in the supernatural. But he also was not unduly impressed by religious demonstrations or their lack in a revival service.

One of the strangest occurrences he witnessed was in Missouri where he was conducting a tent revival. While praying early one day, Lum noticed a huge ball of fire in the air. It moved slowly across town until it was over the main pole of the tent; then it descended the pole and disappeared. Many who were on the street saw the ball of fire. Lum did not mention the incident in the evening service and did not even consider it as having supernatural significance. Nevertheless, the meeting "broke loose" that evening. Sinners screamed for mercy at the mourners' bench, while Christians shouted and ran about, overcome with emotion.

In religious literature there are other accounts of those who witnessed a ball of fire or, in the case of Phineas Bresee, a ball of light. Like Dr. Bresee, Lum Wilson chose to not make this unusual occurrence a part of the gospel message.

7

MISS SARAH

Paducah, Kentucky, June 17 (Special)—Miss Sarah Ragsdale, a well-known young schoolteacher of the city, and Rev. W. C. Wilson, pastor of the M.E. church at Hickory Grove, Graves County, were married here at four o'clock this afternoon.

Lum was becoming better known as W. C. Wilson. He went without a wife for nearly two years. He continued preaching regularly and holding special meetings, although his health was broken and his strength was low. It was in a special meeting in a rural community that a high school principal, Joe Ragsdale, heard him preach several times. Joe mentioned that on Friday night he would bring his sister to the service. When Wilson saw them walk in together that night, he decided at first glance that Sarah would make a wonderful wife. Although she had always said she would never marry a widower or a preacher—and especially not one with children—all that was forgotten as Sarah became attracted to the man on the platform.

Wilson and Sarah were not youngsters swept off their feet by infatuation. Both gave sober, thoughtful consideration to the importance of uniting their lives. To Sarah it meant giving up a prestigious career in teaching. She was a city teacher in Paducah and one of the county examiners for teachers' certificates. The daughter of a Methodist minister, she knew what awaited her in the parsonage, but she never wavered in her decision, even when Wilson hesitated. The contrast between

Eliza, who was large, robust, outgoing, and loudly demonstrative in her religious expressions, and this small, quiet, fashionably dressed schoolteacher made him cautious.

Sarah proved to be the wife he needed. Her education helped him as he furthered his ministerial studies. Her Christian piety was a model to strive for himself.

Sarah's father, Thomas Ragsdale, had lived near the Virginia-North Carolina border before eloping with his bride to Tennessee, where he became a Methodist preacher. During the Civil War he was a Confederate chaplain. After the war was over, life was harder than ever for a Methodist circuit rider in the war-ravished South. The poverty of the ministers and their families was directly responsible for Thomas Ragsdale's death. At age 65 he rode one day from one preaching appointment to another in a bitter, wind-blown, wet snow. He had no overcoat, since he could not afford one, and he became chilled to the bone. He contracted pneumonia and died shortly thereafter.

After her father's death, "Miss Sarah" started teaching school when she was only 15. She secured a teaching certificate by taking an examination and obtained a position at a school where nearby students had forced out earlier teachers. She, however, had no problems with the older boys, who were probably infatuated with her. In spite of the low salaries she and her brothers (also teachers) received, every summer found them improving their professional abilities at Carbondale Normal School, now Southern Illinois University.

All this was given up when she married Wilson, for teaching positions were reserved for widows and single women. Sarah forfeited her own cash income to share her husband's smaller one. Moreover, she had to stretch his income to care for Wilson's children, who had been placed with their mother's relatives at the time of her death and were now returned one by one, and for the children subsequently born to her (Sarah) and Lum.

Marriage was a sacrifice for Sarah, but there was little

worry about groceries. Meat was never in surplus, but food was sufficient. One pound of round steak was a standard for the evening meal, cut into nine small pieces with the last one given to the one who seemed the hungriest. Fried chicken and ice cream were luxuries rarely experienced. Soft drinks and chewing gum were practically unknown.

Monday was always washday, which meant boiling all the clothes and bed linens for the family, wringing them out by hand, rinsing them, wringing them again, rinsing most of them again in bluing water, and again wringing them. Hanging the clothes outdoors—regardless of the weather—was almost relaxing after what had gone on before. On Tuesday nearly everything had to be ironed with irons heated over a coal fire.

Before marriage, Sarah had frequent and prolonged spells of extreme depression, but early in married life she resolutely set out to hide and ignore her feelings of depression. The hard physical labor she endured developed a strong heart and lungs that kept her active until she was 83. In the face of repeated disappointments and tragedies, she was known for her calmness, courage, and cheerfulness.

The first child born to Sarah and Wilson was a son, premature and stillborn. The next two children were honored with being named for Methodist bishops. Bishop Willard F. Mallalieu presided at the annual Methodist conference in Kentucky shortly before little Mallalieu was born. Bishop Fitzgerald held the next conference, and baby Fitzgerald bore his name. She battled for life a few months and gave up.

In gathering the older children back to the fireside, the oldest girl, Bertha Mae, was the logical one to bring first. She was strong and useful, especially in looking after the new babies. After her mother's death, Bertha had been taken in by Eliza's sister, who had become fond of the girl. Bertha was a conscienceless tease who never entirely outgrew her love of practical jokes. She once set the house afire while playing with matches and afterward had a lifelong phobia about fire.

Hallie, the next oldest, had been taken in by her paternal grandparents in Hanson, Kentucky. After Captain Wilson died, the entire family moved in with Grandmother Wilson; and soon little Ruth joined the rest of the family. Only a few months old when her mother died, Ruth had no memory of any home except that of her maternal grandparents, the Gaston Joneses. They lived across the intersection from Grandma Wilson, but even a move of such a short distance was very hard for the little girl. The first night she refused to join the family for the evening meal, but she soon adapted to her new home. She was the most extroverted and cheerful person in the family, friendly with everyone.

Deborah was born to W. C. and Sarah before the children moved in with his widowed mother. William Willard was also born shortly before the move and was named for famous temperance reformer Frances Willard.

Guy was the oldest child of W. C. Wilson and was brought up by his Aunt Henrietta and her husband, Henry Livingstone. He did not rejoin the family until later, after returning home from Asbury College.

This was the existing family circle. Jeanette, the youngest, was not born until after the family left Kentucky and moved to California.

THE HOLINESS REVIVAL IN KENTUCKY

As W. C. Wilson became more successful in revivalism, he received more calls to preach in churches and camp meetings in Kentucky, Georgia, and Alabama. He increasingly associated with leaders of the Holiness Movement, especially those in his native region. Among them were William B. Godbey, Henry Clay Morrison, and L. L. Pickett—all of Kentucky.

Godbey later claimed, and others repeated, that save for John Keen (under whose ministry Wilson was converted), he (Godbey) was the only Holiness preacher in Kentucky Methodism in the early 1880s. A small man, Godbey was a colorful and eccentric preacher and a voluminous writer. Intelligent and self-educated to a high degree of competence, he was sensible on many points but fanatical on others.

Once Godbey and Wilson were holding services together and were lodged in the home of a wealthy church member. Godbey one day grabbed a gallon bucket, dashed to the street, bought a bucket of buttermilk, and returned upstairs, sloshing milk on the expensive rugs. Wilson reproved him, but Godbey's dismissive reply was "Brother Wilson, you should be dead to such things." Not being so "dead," Wilson took a rag and sponged the mess as well as possible.

For both good and bad, Godbey's influence permeated the Southern Holiness Movement. He preached a thoroughly un-Methodist version of premillennialism (dispensationalism). He predicted the second coming of Christ by 1923 at the latest. He rejected the King James Version of the Bible and made a translation of the New Testament that he considered superior because he used newly discovered biblical manuscripts that were more ancient than those used by the KJV translators. His theological legacy was mixed.

Another Kentucky Holiness preacher was Henry Clay Morrison, who was ostracized by the Southern Methodist hierarchy after entering Holiness evangelism. In 1896 he was expelled from the Methodist ministry for conducting a Holiness revival in Texas without the approval of the local parish pastor. Morrison had violated church law, but he fought back so vigorously, if not viciously, that on appeal his credentials were restored on a technicality.

As editor of the *Pentecostal Herald,* Morrison gave the Holiness Movement an effective voice throughout Kentucky and the South. He moved to Wilmore, Kentucky, and led a group of outstanding Holiness evangelists centered there. He was president of Asbury College, a strong bastion of Southern Holiness, for many years.

Another friend of Wilson at Wilmore was L. L. Pickett, whose son later became a Methodist bishop. Pickett was a warrior of the same type as Morrison, without the same stature. *The Pickett-Smith Debate* was a book in Wilson's library containing verbatim a public debate on sanctification between Pickett and a Church of Christ minister. Wilson believed, however, that his friend was clearly defeated in this famous contest. Pickett used an analogy popular among Holiness preachers. He compared conversion to a tree being felled and entire sanctification to digging up the stump of sin. When Smith asked Pickett to explain why some sanctified people showed traits contrary to their profession, Pickett replied that after a stump is removed, there are still roots left in the ground that will send up sprouts and must be cut down. Smith gleefully pounced on this as supporting *his* side of the argument, namely that not all sin is eradicated by the second blessing. Wilson believed that the doctrine of holiness rested on Scripture and Christian experience, not on an analogy.

In his own ministry, Wilson had encountered no serious opposition to his Holiness preaching or his antiliquor and antitobacco messages until 1903, when he held a revival at the Baptist church in his hometown of Hanson, Kentucky. Holiness preachers were speaking out against tobacco as "filthiness of the flesh" (2 Cor. 7:1), and their point of view was accepted later when Southern Methodists prohibited further admission of tobacco users into their ordained ministry. In 1903 the attack against tobacco was economic heresy in Kentucky. Even as Wilson held a revival in the Baptist church in Hanson, local Southern Methodists were meeting weekly in a tobacco factory, owned by one of their members, while the church building was remodeled.

Alcoholic beverages were a similar issue, though many Kentuckians were teetotalers even before joining a church. Indeed, a temperance society was formed in the state well before the Civil War, and drunkenness often led to dismissal from churches.

At the time the Wilson family moved to Hanson, Wilson himself withdrew from the Methodist Episcopal Church and made plans to unite with the Methodist Episcopal Church, South. He explained to friends that the decision was made because there was no Methodist Episcopal congregation in Hanson. There was another reason as well, however. The Methodist Episcopal Church was trying hard to compete with the Methodist Episcopal Church, South. While the Methodist Episcopal Church was much larger nationally, the Methodist Episcopal Church, South, dominated Methodism in the Southern states. In Kentucky the Southern denomination had larger and more numerous congregations, which gave an evangelist greater opportunity. Moreover, he did not want to spend his life helping the Northern church compete with its Southern sister. His credentials could not be transferred until the annual meeting of the conference, however. In order to continue his ministry, Wilson resigned from the Methodist Episcopal ministry and joined the Southern Methodist congregation in Hanson with the status of a layman. He obtained a local preacher's license, which was used as his authority to preach until the annual conference.

Wilson had never conducted a revival in his home community, so he assented when friends and relatives invited him to do so in the Baptist church across the street from his mother's house. In accordance with Methodist church law, Wilson asked permission of the local Southern Methodist pastor to conduct a religious meeting within the latter's parish. Wilson maintained later that permission was given him in writing, but the pastor denied it.

Some facts were not in dispute. The pastor urged Wilson to cancel the meeting. Failing that, he urged the Baptists to withdraw use of their building. They did not, and the revival meetings began on a Sunday. On Tuesday, the pastor attended the meeting and sat in the back, and Wilson called on him to lead in prayer. After the service, the pastor confronted Wilson and told him never to call on him again until the authority of the Methodist pastor to take charge of the meeting was recognized. On Saturday, the presiding elder (superintendent) of the district came and urged Wilson to halt the revival. They discussed it but came to no agreement. When it was time for the service to begin, Wilson went directly to the church and preached.

The revival was a success, with the house packed and scores converted. But Wilson was placed on church trial for holding a revival not duly authorized. Several years earlier, Henry Clay Morrison successfully fought his expulsion from the ministry over the same issue, but Southern Methodist law had been tightened since then. Now no local preacher was allowed to conduct religious services when requested not to do so by the bishop-appointed minister. Wilson was found guilty, his local preacher's license was revoked, and he was ordered to desist from preaching.

As soon as the trial ended, Wilson rode home with Sarah, packed his valise, whipped up the horse, and went to conduct his next revival. Two young men converted in that meeting later became Methodist ministers. By ignoring the instructions of the church court, Wilson forfeited his right to appeal the verdict. He was determined to preach holiness, but now he was without a church home. Although he might have been able to rejoin the Methodist Episcopal Church by canceling the transfer he had arranged from the Northern body, he apparently gave no consideration to this course.

Wilson was urgently invited by his friend J. O. McClurkan to unite with the Pentecostal Mission in Nashville. The Pentecostal Mission boasted Trevecca College, a connectional paper, and a reputation for being the best-organized Holiness work in the upper South. Affiliated congregations were expanding rapidly in all sections of the Southeast.

Two things prevented Wilson from joining: McClurkan's followers emphasized divine healing of the body as a major tenet, and they insisted on premillennialism as the only true view of the Second Coming. Also, the work was centered around the charismatic personality of McClurkan. Wilson questioned the permanence of the Pentecostal Mission's efforts, since it lacked a solid denominational form. He could not foresee that McClurkan would take steps to correct this and that one day the Pentecostal Mission and the Wilson family would be united in the Pentecostal Church of the Nazarene.

There were other options. The Church of God (Anderson, Indiana) was a definite Holiness church, but it was opposed on principle to denominationalism. This was not Wilson's conviction. Across the Ohio River in Cincinnati, Martin Wells Knapp, a former Methodist Episcopal minister, headed an impressive Holiness work centered around God's Bible School and the *Revivalist,* a popular periodical. However, Knapp died about this time, and leadership of the group was unsettled. (It later became the main branch of the Pilgrim Holiness Church.)

Wilson also considered organizing bands of independent Holiness people into their own church. In Madisonville, Kentucky, there was such a band, and shortly after the break with the Southern Methodists, the Wilson family moved there. The Holiness band met in homes on Sunday afternoons and on weeknights for prayer meetings.

Then Wilson contacted Rev. C. W. Ruth, a noted evangelist from Indianapolis who had united two years earlier with the Church of the Nazarene in Los Angeles. Ruth had become the assistant general superintendent of this new Holiness denomination, which was still largely centered on the West Coast. Ruth replied by recommending the Nazarenes highly, and he appealed to Wilson with the statement that the Nazarenes were "nothing in the world but old-fashioned Methodism, with a congregational form of government." Ruth noted that like the early Methodists, "our business is to spread scriptural holiness over these lands."*

Wilson took Ruth's advice and wrote to Dr. Bresee. He received an encouraging reply from Bresee and a copy of the church's *Manual*. He liked what he read. As a result, the older members of the Wilson family were accepted into the membership of the Los Angeles First Church of the Nazarene. Wilson still had the ordination credential issued when he was ordained in the Methodist Episcopal Church. He now received a certificate of recognition as an elder in the Church of the Nazarene. It was dated October 3, 1903, and was signed by Phineas Bresee.

---

*MS letter of C. W. Ruth to "W. C. Wilson and Wife," August 3, 1903. In the William C. Wilson Collection, Nazarene Archives.

9

A NEW CHURCH HOME

In March 1905, Wilson conducted a meeting in the Second Methodist Episcopal Church of Princeton, Indiana, when the opportunity came to talk with Rev. C. E. Cornell, who was holding a meeting in another Methodist church in town. Cornell was also a Nazarene minister, and the two men talked about the young denomination to which they belonged. The Church of the Nazarene in 1905 still had its center of gravity along the Pacific coast, but it was beginning to grow outside its native region and expand eastward. Indeed, Cornell would shortly become pastor of Chicago First Church of the Nazarene. He had conducted a revival for Bresee two years earlier at Los Angeles First Church and knew the West Coast leaders personally. Wilson knew much about Bresee and the work in the West through the church paper, the *Nazarene Messenger,* but he had never visited the vital centers of Nazarene life as Cornell had done.

Wilson's next meeting was in McLeansboro, Illinois, where previously he had ended a successful meeting. Now the prohibition forces wanted him back during the local election, because the licensing of saloons was a controversial public issue. Wilson spoke out forcefully against the saloons and gathered crowds too large to be seated in any building in town. The offerings were quite liberal.

Wilson's next meeting was canceled, and he had unexpected time and cash. He used the opportunity to go west and meet Dr. Bresee. Instead of traveling directly to Los Angeles, he went by way of Salt Lake City; Nampa, Idaho; Portland, Oregon; and San Francisco, enjoying the vast new area and carefully considering each place as a future home. He visited Dr. Bresee shortly after arriving in Los Angeles and found they were in substantial accord on a broad range of issues.

Bresee was a strong believer in the local church and was looking for strong pastors. Wilson recognized that evangelism was not enough—that unless those who experience conversion and entire sanctification are rooted in a church body where they are accountable for their holy walk, then they can drift spiritually. Both men disdained the divisions among Holiness people—disagreements over the Second Coming, divine healing, and dress. Both believed that the one thing to emphasize is holiness of heart and life and that other issues were secondary to the spread of scriptural holiness. At the close of their conversation, Bresee and Wilson knelt in prayer and rejoiced together as two kindred souls that had met.

In a few days the two men visited Upland, California, together, where an all-day meeting was taking place. Wilson preached in the afternoon, using Heb. 2:11 as his text: "For both he that sanctifieth and they who are sanctified are all of one: for which cause he is not ashamed to call them brethren." He then preached at Los Angeles First Church the following Sunday morning and began a tent meeting at Long Beach the following week. There were over 100 seekers in the tent meeting, and on May 29 a church was organized in Long Beach with 30 charter members. Wilson was called unanimously as pastor and accepted the invitation.

He wrote Sarah to prepare the family for a move to California. Excitedly, she told the children, "Let's sell the furniture and pack before he changes his mind!"

Everyone went to work eagerly. Handbills announcing a sale were printed and distributed. Price tags were put on nearly everything in the house, and on the appointed day the sale was a complete success.

Things were packed to be shipped west by freight. This included Sarah's *Encyclopaedia Britannica,* Webster's dictionary, professional books, and all of Wilson's ministerial library.

Then Wilson sent a message from California stating that he was disappointed and planned to return to Kentucky in a few weeks. Sarah sent word back that it was too late—they had sold out, packed up, and would be in California soon.

After shipping the freight, the family spent a few days visiting relatives and then regathered in Madisonville, where they boarded the train west. Guy carried the tickets and schedules. Sarah carried Willard, who was only two. Ruth carried eight feather pillows strapped into two bulky bundles. Bertha and Hallie carried the lunch—about two bushels of food, including sandwiches, cakes, cookies, and fried chicken. Mallalieu and Deborah were at the tender ages where they were expected to carry themselves and nothing more. To St. Louis, Kansas City, Denver, Salt Lake City, and finally Los Angeles—the trip began on Monday evening and ended the following Sunday morning.

W. C. Wilson met them in Los Angeles early in the day and traveled with his family to Long Beach. They all sat in the front seats of a schoolroom later that morning, and the children looked up with faces shining with pride as their father preached to his congregation. Afterward, the cool green lawns and trees of Long Beach seemed like a veritable Garden of Eden to this family who had spent a week on a smoky, dusty train crossing the great American desert in the hot summer.

On Monday night an informal reception was held at the parsonage, a four-room house about two blocks from the schoolhouse. After Wilson decided to rent it, a man who was not a church member raised donations to furnish the cottage. The congregation responded well, providing plain but sturdy furniture.

Once summer ended and school began, church services were moved from the school building to a rented hall farther downtown. Later, a different hall was leased near the first. In one of these halls a Pentecostal congregation rented the second floor directly above the Nazarenes. Noisy competition erupted until the Pentecostals finally found another meeting place.

In October the annual assembly of the Church of the Nazarene was held in Los Angeles. This event was more of a Holiness convention than a district or general assembly. Wilson preached on Wednesday night and again the following Tuesday. Sunday was the big day, and the Long Beach congregation attended together.

At this assembly, members of the Upland congregation approached Wilson about becoming their pastor. Unlike Long Beach, Upland had a church building that was nearly completed. He accepted and became the first pastor called by the Upland Church of the Nazarene.

The Wilson family moved to this community in the autumn of 1905. Furniture was hauled in two horse-drawn wagons furnished by Jackson Deets, a member of the Upland congregation. It took two days for the stoutest draft horses to pull a wagon from Long Beach to Upland, 60 miles away, so the family took the train. Upon arrival, the Wilsons stayed awhile with the Deets family in their home.

Upland-Ontario seemed like one of the most uniformly beautiful small communities in the world. Water from the melting snows of Mount San Antonio sustained an oasis about one mile wide and seven miles long. Almost without exception, all land not actually used for dwellings or other types of trees was planted with evergreen navel orange trees, with their dark foliage reaching to the ground all around, or lemon trees with their lighter green leaves.

Euclid Avenue ran from the valley floor to the foothills—a double highway divided by a wide parkway with two rows of ornamental pepper trees. The lower end of Euclid, where the Southern Pacific and the Salt Lake railroads crossed the oasis, was the business center of Ontario. The Santa Fe crossed two miles up the grade. The business district of Upland was above the Santa Fe, and the Nazarene church was one block north of the Santa Fe station on Main and Ninth.

Ontario was well-churched, including a Nazarene congregation pastored by A. O. Hendricks, a dynamic and likable young pastor. By contrast, Upland had only three good-sized churches and the new Church of the Nazarene. The largest church was the "River Brethren," or Brethren in Christ, who shared the Nazarene emphasis on John Wesley's doctrine of entire sanctification. Nazarenes and Brethren cooperated in revivals and conventions, and many Nazarenes were related to Brethren families. The Methodist church was only a few blocks from the Nazarene church. The Methodists did not cooperate closely with Nazarenes like the Brethren, but they were friendly on a personal basis. The Presbyterians had no feeling of rivalry with the Nazarenes. Their pastor, also a native Kentuckian, once dismissed his Sunday night service and brought his congregation to the Nazarene church for the closing night of the revival.

Wilson rented a house for his family on Eighth Street near Euclid Avenue. Between them and Euclid Avenue was a vacant lot where they planted a winter crop of grain for cow and chicken feed. Wilson was also an expert beekeeper, and as people discovered this, they called on him to rid their houses and yards of unwelcome swarms. He upgraded the colonies by purchasing Italian queens and dividing colonies before they could swarm. He soon had choice honey to sell, as well as a liberal supply for the family table.

Wilson's youngest daughter, Jeanette, was born during his first year at Upland. During that time Bertha enrolled in Pacific Bible College (later known as Pasadena College and Point Loma Nazarene College) in Los Angeles, where Guy was already attending. Throughout that first year Wilson was occupied with pastoral duties. However, he found time to assist in a revival in Cucamonga in February and conduct some all-day meetings in nearby towns at other times. In April he preached at the dedication of the Long Beach church's new building, and in June he oversaw the installation of new pews in the Upland church.

Sometime in 1906, a conversation with Jackson Deets precipitated another family move. Deets knew of a reasonably priced lemon ranch that was available. Wilson could never have afforded it, no matter how good a bargain, but Deets loaned the necessary amount, and Wilson owned property again for the first time since selling his Kentucky farm to enter the ministry some 20 years previous.

The Wilsons did not even own a horse, but after moving to the lemon ranch, they borrowed one several days each month. Wilson rode a bicycle to pastoral appointments, which was fine except when he hit the steep north grade. With an increasing load of church work, one year of pedaling a bike was all he could stand. Deets again came to the rescue, buying the ranch for double its price of the year before.

The profit from the lemon ranch was used for a down payment on a two-acre site with young orange trees and an improved house closer to town. The new home demanded less work and usually furnished a net profit from the sale of fruit to supplement Wilson's salary. (The Upland congregation eventually constructed a new church building on the adjoining acreage and still later bought the two acres itself for a parking lot and gave the house to a Hispanic congregation.)

During Wilson's pastorate at Upland, the Church of the Nazarene began some early mission work. Wilson agreed with Bresee's philosophy of building a strong home base before expanding into foreign missions, but opportunities presented themselves in India and Japan. Both were initiated by consecrated laywomen.

Sukhoda Banarjee, a converted Hindu widow, was traveling down the Pacific coast in 1906 with her nephew and Mrs. Emma Eaton, who was from Oregon. The San Francisco earthquake caused them to change their itinerary, and they decided to visit Dr. Bresee in Los Angeles. Afterward, they toured Nazarene churches in southern California, including Upland. Mrs. Banarjee and her nephew returned to India with the official support of the Church of the Nazarene. Mrs. Eaton and her husband went to India some months later as Nazarene missionaries.

Almost one year later, another future missionary came to Upland. The husband of Minnie Staples was transferred to the Santa Fe station as a telegrapher. After being in Upland a short time, Mrs. Staples became concerned for a group that was shunned and almost totally ignored: the men of the Japanese labor camp. These men did practically all the fruit picking for the community and did so at the lowest wages. Mrs. Staples worked diligently among the Japanese on the West Coast and eventually became a missionary in Japan, obtaining a remarkable fluency in Japanese. Wilson appreciated Mrs. Staples's work. As her pastor and later her district superintendent, he was her favorite counselor.

10

THE CHURCH GROWS

During Wilson's Upland pastorate, the Church of the Nazarene became part of a wider ministry outside the Los Angeles area. In 1907 it affiliated with the Association of Pentecostal Churches of America, another Holiness group located largely in New England, New York State, and Pennsylvania. The merger of the two churches formed a larger denomination known for many years as the Pentecostal Church of the Nazarene. Wilson played a prominent role in this union as one of three members on the negotiating committee who represented the Church of the Nazarene. The other two members from the West were General Superintendent P. F. Bresee and Assistant General Superintendent C. W. Ruth.

The work of the Upland church went on steadily. Economic pressures generated by the financial "Panic of 1907" were among the problems that had to be faced. Money was tight and unemployment was common during the panic. The church found various ministry opportunities during this time. An unemployed man who drifted up to the Wilson farm from the railroad was given a square meal in exchange for chores. When Wilson discovered that the vagrant was a Christian man from Los Angeles, he helped him find work in the Upland area and arranged for his family to join him. This family later became members of the Church of the Nazarene.

Wilson also cautioned wealthier members of his congregation about their labor practices. Because the labor pool swelled steadily, some employers saw an opportunity to cut the wages they were paying in order to increase profits. There were few unions to protect laborers at the time, but Wilson advised employers in his congregation that reducing wages at the expense of workers simply to realize larger profits was not an appropriate Christian response during a time that was financially difficult for workers.

Under Wilson's ministry, revivals were a frequent part of the Upland church's life. Many special speakers came. S. B. Rhodes preached on dedication Sunday and returned on New Year's Day to hold special meetings. Revivals could be up to three weeks long, like the one conducted the very next month by E. A. Ross. Only one month later, Carrie Crow and Lulu Kell started yet another meeting. As their example showed, Wilson was not opposed to women preachers. The two women were, in fact, friends of his from Kentucky days and had entered the ministry with his encouragement. Minnie Staples was another special speaker who came, and Lulu Rogers of Texas was called to conduct a revival at Upland in February 1908. Wilson's support of these women surely influenced his daughter, Bertha, who would one day follow him into the ministry and pastor Indianapolis First Church. His oldest son, Guy, was also a frequent guest preacher at the Upland church.

The annual Sunday School picnic was a big event in the life of early California Nazarenes. Bresee's congregation in Los Angeles and some Nazarene churches in nearby towns had made it a practice to hold all-day meetings at the beach. They had church services before and after lunch, and then a baptismal service was sometimes held in the ocean for new converts. Following this, all who wished to swim in the surf and "jump the waves" were welcome to do so. Upland had no water for swimming, but the Nazarene church there observed the annual picnic nonetheless.

(Note: The church *Manual* never did forbid "mixed bathing," although a resolution in the 1928 *Manual* does mention it.)

In September 1907, Wilson went east to hold revival meetings and attend the first General Assembly at Chicago, at which the church union was to be consummated in October. His first meeting was at Irvington, Kentucky, where his brother Ben was pastor of the Methodist church. Before he could go on to Chicago, however, he received the dismaying news that his daughter Hallie had been struck down with typhoid fever—the very disease that had taken the life of her mother. Wilson went immediately back to Upland, stopping in Hanson, Kentucky, to pick up his mother. Hallie did not die, and a trained nurse moved in to look after her during the most critical time of her illness. Her recovery took many months.

In spite of the troubles experienced by the Wilson family, the church ended the year in good shape. The Christmas program attracted the largest attendance ever, and growth continued in 1908. In April, Sunday School attendance reached a new high of 102.

Wilson took his mother back to Kentucky in May. He stopped in Wilmore to see Guy, who was enrolled at Asbury College. In June, he and Martha Curry, a Nazarene revivalist from the East, were preachers at the Beulah Park Camp Meeting in northern California, near San Francisco Bay. There were 200 seekers, including two ministers from other denominations.

At the district assembly in August 1908, Upland reported 80 members, among a total district membership of about 2,000. Nearly half were members of a single congregation—Los Angeles First Church. The directory of evangelists published earlier that year in the *Nazarene Messenger* listed fewer than a dozen names. At that time, there were 18 Nazarene churches in southern California.

11

PASADENA

In 1908 W. C. Wilson resigned from the church at Upland and again became pastor at Long Beach. The Long Beach congregation now had its own building on Seventh Street. The family resided only a mile from the ocean, where Wilson enjoyed swimming in the cold water and diving under the big breakers. Sometimes he took the children to the hot salt-water plunge, where he delighted in going down the slide and diving from the springboard and platform. He also liked to fish. A few times he went out in a boat, but usually he fished from the wharf. Yellowtail and barracuda were not uncommon, and there were always mackerel around.

Wilson's second pastorate at Long Beach lasted only eight months. He was persuaded to return briefly to Upland as interim pastor, serving from April through June. His previous successor at Upland had come from the Methodist church. Apparently his wife wore a feather in her hat, which provoked controversy. Wilson filled the pulpit at Upland until U. E. Ramsey from Indiana was called as the new permanent pastor.

That summer Wilson preached at camp meetings in the Midwest. He reported good meetings at Water Valley, Kentucky; the Eldorado Camp in Illinois, where he shared the pulpit with his friend Carrie Crow; and at Stanford, Illinois, where he closed "with a sweep of victory."

Church services, both regular and evangelistic, were lively. "Amen," "Bless God," "Hallelujah," "Praise the Lord," and "Glory" could be heard from the moment people entered the service until the benediction was pronounced. Most members, however, expressed their feelings with only a smile. Wilson believed in freedom of expression in religious services, but he did not hesitate to cut off anyone who tried to pray too long, speak too long, or shout too long. Usually this was done by "singing him down." Wilson may have lacked ability as a soloist, but he had a strong voice and never needed a microphone to be heard over the crowd.

In those early years there were no missionary budgets, educational budgets, or, in fact, any budgets at all. Funds were raised by truly freewill offerings. There was little systematic giving, even for current local expenses. As the denomination acquired campgrounds, colleges, publishing houses, and mission projects, however, it became harder to be so carefree about money. Wilson was among the first pastors to introduce the weekly envelope system. He tithed and encouraged the idea that tithes should be given to the local church because it needed them to survive.

In 1909 Wilson moved his family to Pasadena to pastor the First Church of the Nazarene. He inherited a church with a crushing debt. The congregation was started in 1905 by John W. Goodwin, later general superintendent. In less than two years Goodwin had built the church membership to 80 and secured a building on the corner of Fair Oaks and Mary Street costing $20,000. In the two years after Goodwin left, other pastors came and went. None were able to hold up the membership or cut the debt. In the year before Wilson's arrival, Sunday School attendance had not been more than 65. Under his ministry, however, attendance was raised to more than 100, and within two years the debt was oversubscribed.

Pasadena First Church had a core of strong, dependable members who were, for the most part, Holiness people from Methodism. There were many other good people, but from such widely varying religious and cultural backgrounds that building them into a united group demanded pastoral diplomacy. Wilson was very aware of how necessary love and tolerance are in order for people to build a truly Holiness church. In other churches he often preached sanctification on Sunday mornings, but at Pasadena First nearly all the members professed the experience of entire sanctification. Wilson took opportunity one Sunday to speak about the varied backgrounds of church members. Some had already changed denominations several times and were restless with the church program. They liked to attend where there was shouting and where singing was free and hilarious, but they disliked teaching Sunday School or paying bills. Other members were interested in mission work in the slums, where drunks could be sobered and prostitutes dramatically transformed, but they did not appreciate the necessity of a church home for Christians of that background after they were converted.

There were those who considered immersion necessary for salvation as well as those who believed in only Spirit baptism. Several families had lingering beliefs in "soul sleep" after death. Some members liked the brass-band type of service, and some opposed all instrumental music in worship. There was one group influenced by a "fourfold gospel" emphasizing conversion, baptism of the Holy Spirit, divine healing, and premillennialism. And then there was the core congregation made up of former Methodists. All these factions brought diversity to the church, although sanctifying grace was sometimes necessary to harmonize the differences.

During this period, speaking in tongues was an issue in the churches of southern California. The members of Pasadena Grace Church, a black Nazarene church, always enjoyed an emotional style of worship that was Pentecostal in tone. Eventually the congregation and its pastor became tongues advocates and requested permission to withdraw from the Pentecostal Church of the Nazarene. On Wilson's recommendation, the district granted the request, and the church was on its own.

Wilson never preached outright against those who believed in tongues-speaking. He thought the best way to compete with them was to outsing, outpray, and outshout them. That was the philosophy shared by C. E. Cornell a few years later when popular revivalist Aimee Semple McPherson started the Angelus Temple in downtown Los Angeles, drawing many people from Los Angeles First Church, where Cornell was pastor. He refused to attack Sister Aimee, though preachers in many other denominations were doing so. Instead, he urged his people to be faithful to their own churches, saying, "Anything God has for you, you can seek and find at this altar," and again, "Put your money in our offering plates here. We will send it wherever you want it to go. If you mark an envelope for Aimee, we'll see that she gets it." Most of the sheep listened and before long returned to the fold.

Wilson was aggressively evangelistic in his pastoral personality, and he was comparable to C. E. Cornell and A. O. Hendricks, peers and district leaders who also pastored Pasadena First Church at some point. However, Wilson did not consider evangelistic emphasis a matter of frequent special meetings or conventions. He was outspoken in his belief that a church needed only one special revival effort each year, although he sometimes had meetings more frequently. He believed in the type of preaching that brought unbelievers to conversion and believers into entire sanctification. He believed in preaching with a definite goal. He did not expect sinners to repent after hearing a sermon on entire sanctification, nor did he expect Christians to seek a second work of grace when he had preached on repentance. In either case he depended on the sermon to produce the conviction that moved people to decision rather than prolonged, emotional altar calls with sentimental songs.

Wilson worked on his sermons all week and discussed at the table or in family prayers the reading he had been doing. He rarely wrote a sermon manuscript, nor did he take notes into the pulpit. Like most of the early Holiness preachers, Wilson preached forcefully. He had a powerful voice but did not yell. He preached in a conversational tone that could be heard and understood by anyone, with the only variations being occasional shouts of laughter and exclamations—especially, "Well, glory!" He never pounded the pulpit or ran from one end of the platform to the other, but he used gestures and other types of nonverbal communication to reinforce his messages, which were always sensible and practical.

Wilson was not a high-pressure type of minister. There were unconverted men who attended his church for years without ever professing any religion, but he never embarrassed them by singling them out for attention during an altar call. When he was with them outside the church, he did not feel it his constant duty to rebuke them for their sins. One man, who was alcoholic, liked to fish with Wilson, but the pastor did not use the occasion to lecture. He fished. The man did not immediately repent of his ways, which he knew were evil, but he was finally converted and died with triumphant victory. His widow was convinced that it was Wilson's fishing trips and friendliness that were responsible for her husband's salvation and reformation. And eventually all these men were converted, attributing their conversions to the patient friendship that the pastor had shown them.

Wilson's gracious attitude did not stem from timidity or extend to men who neglected or abused their families. He could be most fearlessly outspoken in his blistering condemnation of such men. He was similarly rough in his treatment of arrogant critics of Christian people. Ordinary sinners he loved, but he had no use for pompous, conceited braggarts or brutal characters.

Wilson enjoyed visiting with businessmen, neighbors, and people of other denominations, but at the same time he was faithful in his regular pastoral visitation (although he sometimes felt this was drudgery). He was also emphatic about this being an absolute essential of successful pastoral ministry.

In church finances he was cautious about unnecessary involvement in debt, but he encouraged optimistic generosity. On the other hand, he realized that faith was often increased by seeing visible results.

Wilson was aggressively evangelistic in Pasadena as elsewhere, but his program did not include starting new churches or moving the church to a new and "more central" location. In his first year at Pasadena he rented a tent and pitched it on the corner of Chester and Colorado streets, which at that time was near the eastern edge of the city. Wilson did most of the preaching in this meeting, and many people came to the tent who had never been in the church. At least one family joined the church as a direct result of finding the experience of entire sanctification in the meeting. No new church was necessary, for anyone could ride the electric cars for five cents from any place in the city and arrive almost at the doors of the church.

Wilson never tried to lay down a pattern of devotional life for other people. He greatly admired Sarah's habit of rising early for a leisurely reading of Scripture and private prayer before starting the day's work, but such a program never suited his temperament. Sarah tended to take everything slowly and calmly, and she might go all day and until after midnight before being ready to retire. Wilson was impatient to get going and, traveling as he did much of the time, rarely could follow any detailed schedule for two successive days. But he exemplified the three admonitions printed on his letterhead: "Be Prompt. Be Prayerful. Be Courteous."

Wilson believed that praying and working were so bound up that he could not conceive of a person losing his spirituality while he was behaving as he should and doing the Lord's work. He did not need a long period of leisure to get blessed. He could come in from pruning a lemon tree and shout, "Glory! Hallelujah!" as sincerely as if he had spent many hours alone in his study. He never tolerated any kind of rarefied "spirituality" that supposedly was only for the cloistered few and was not practicable for laymen.

Wilson considered prayer the key to successful evangelistic meetings. Before a series of such meetings, he would have special prayer meetings held in homes. These were never whole nights of prayer, for his members were mostly workingmen or mothers of small children. He stressed faith rather than much speaking and set an example of faith that was contagious.

12

THE FAMILY MATURES

Family life for the Wilsons was typical of most preachers' families in the early days of the Church of the Nazarene. Few churches owned parsonages, which was fortunate for the Wilsons, for they would have had difficulty crowding into a parsonage built for the average preacher's family. Wilson always tried to rent a large, two-story house that was roomy rather than one that was convenient or modern in appearance. Their first Pasadena home was on Lincoln Avenue, just a few blocks from the church. The second was on Cypress Avenue. It was even larger, and it had a barn with a large overhead hayloft. In dry weather some family members occasionally slept upstairs on the roofless porch.

Grocery stores were beginning to advertise "specials" on large sheets of paper, with the names and prices of products splashed on in red and blue. Wilson grew quite interested in this and tried the technique on a bulletin board in front of the church. It had no effect on church attendance, but the grocery ads did change family life. Wilson began bringing home foods his family had never eaten before. Large quantities of stew meat, prepared cereals, bakery bread and cakes, and new vegetables and fruits became more common on the table.

The Pasadena years were decisive for the family, especially for the older children. The older daughters were engaged and married during this period.

Guy, the oldest son, had moved to California with the family, but he lived with them for only a few weeks at Long Beach before leaving to attend Pacific Bible College in Los Angeles. This was the school that became Pasadena College and is now Point Loma Nazarene College, in San Diego. Dr. Bresee was its president. Guy went on to earn a degree in theology from Asbury College in Wilmore, Kentucky—the leading educational institution of the Wesleyan-Holiness movement in that day. He became an evangelist for a time, then settled into pastoring the Nazarene church in Berkeley, California. Guy had many connections in Kentucky, particularly among Methodists, and he soon returned to revivalism, focusing his work in the Midwest and East.

In 1913 Guy married Gaynell Kimball, a tall, stately woman from Maine. In time, he reunited with the Methodist Church and continued holding revivals for nearly 18 years. Often he preached alongside "Uncle" Bud Robinson. Finally, he joined the Maine Conference of the Methodist Church and was a pastor until retiring 24 years later. From his father, Guy learned to be a strong preacher, dramatic and oratorical. When his father died leaving unpaid debts, Guy assumed responsibility for them and paid them off over several years.

Bertha was the oldest daughter. She was a senior at Pacific Bible College when her family moved to Pasadena. They saw her very little, since she was part of a college singing group that traveled to churches on weekends. In one of the groups there was a singer named Haldor Lillenas, a Norwegian immigrant. When summer came, he called on Bertha at her home, and the family could hear them in the parlor singing and playing the piano. They decided to marry the following summer. Haldor did not have a regular job, but he had saved over $100 from various sources, including the proceeds from songs he had written and sold.

Bertha and Haldor married in 1910 and moved to Sacramento, where they took charge of the Peniel Mission. After a year they became pastors of a Nazarene church. Both were ordained ministers, and their joint ministry of preaching and song lasted for 35 years, until Bertha died of cancer in 1945.

As Haldor gave increasing attention to music, Bertha took more of the preaching responsibility. They were pastoring Indianapolis First Church together when Haldor decided to leave the pastoral ministry and start a gospel music company. Bertha continued to pastor the congregation by herself for several more years until the general church bought Lillenas Music Company and moved it, and them, to Kansas City.

Bertha was a more emotional preacher than her father, but she was poised and graceful. She found it easy to weep as she preached or sang, but she did not shout, "Glory! Hallelujah!" as W. C. Wilson did. Her father was profoundly pleased with her and his son-in-law, and he was grateful that they were with him at the 1915 General Assembly that elected him to the general superintendency of the church.

Hallie Wilson was a family favorite and had the character of a saint. She recorded the date of her conversion on the flyleaf of her New Testament a few days after her 10th birthday. Two years later she entered the date of her sanctification experience. After fighting typhoid fever when she was 16, Hallie's ambitions usually exceeded her strength, which often waned. Of all her suitors, she favored only George J. Franklin. They married and moved to a little house in a canyon near the Olinda Church of the Nazarene, which he pastored. The congregation and salary were small, but even economies and makeshifts seemed to delight Hallie.

Six months after her marriage, Hallie died. Her father was never the same after her death, and he wrote in his diary that he sometimes wished to slip away to heaven, where Hallie had gone. Hallie's husband was overwhelmed by the loss and feared that the Wilson family would lose interest in him. They never did. George Franklin became a missionary in India and there married Hulda Grebe, a classmate from Pacific Bible College. George and Hulda were treated like brothers and sisters by Hallie's siblings and were always considered a part of the family.

Ruth, the youngest child of Eliza and W. C. Wilson, was still a baby when her mother died and was raised by grandparents until she was 10. She had returned unwillingly to the Wilson family but had adapted cheerfully, as she did to every situation. Ruth grew into a pretty girl and was popular with boys, which worried her father excessively and unnecessarily. She married Charles Orrin, 10 years her senior, a carpenter and longtime member of Pasadena First Church. She survived one misfortune after another with seeming cheerfulness and steadfastness.

While the older children were marrying and starting new lives, the four younger ones were still in school. Pasadena was their home for many years.

Mallalieu was the only Wilson child to graduate from Pasadena College (formerly Pacific Bible College). He entered the United States Army and in 1919 married his high school and college classmate, Jewell McNeill. They became teachers and served at four Nazarene colleges. Mallalieu also spent five years as a pastor in California, serving Nazarene churches at Vallejo and Bakersfield.

Deborah graduated from Pasadena Academy, the high school attached for many years to Pasadena College. She married Arthur Grobe, a Canadian, and joined him in pastoral ministry in Canada, California, and the Midwest.

Willard's talents were in music and writing. He sold his first story for $20 while in junior high school—the beginning of a literary career that included a Ph.D. in English literature and 39 years at the University of Hawaii, where he was a professor, dean of students, dean of arts and sciences, dean of faculties, provost, and acting president. He was described by others as erudite and urbane.

Jeanette, or Janet, as she preferred to be called, was the youngest child, and the only member of the family to spend her entire life in California. She was only nine when her father died. She was talented musically and spent her time studying piano and organ after graduating from high school. She married a pressman and printer named Worth Runquist and had her own business for several years.

The impact of W. C. Wilson's personality on his children was evident in that five of eight sons and daughters were either ministers or minister's spouses. There have continued to be ministers in each succeeding generation of the family. In 1991 Larry Wilson was ordained an elder, and his wife, Martha, was ordained a deacon on the New England District—the fourth generation of Wilsons to be ordained to the Christian ministry in the Church of the Nazarene.

13

INFLUENCING A YOUNG DENOMINATION

Pacific Bible College's name was changed to Nazarene University on June 8, 1906. Deets Pacific Bible College was one of its departments. W. C. Wilson was among the trustees to oversee the school under its new charter. Jackson Deets, the family friend from Upland, was another. Deets donated a tract of land in Hollywood for the new campus, and in his honor the religion department's new name reflected his gift.

The new campus was still a hayfield when the dedication service was held. Part of the tract donated by Deets had been subdivided into lots, and these were sold to secure money for buildings. Deets promised the school $20,000 if the church would raise $30,000. This was thinking on a grand scale. Bresee remarked in a board meeting: "Brother Deets proposes to make this the greatest Bible college in the world." By the following year there were 20 students enrolled. In 1907 Guy Wilson and Percy Girvin were the two graduates.

Troubles developed, however. The financial panic of 1907 slowed the sale of lots, reducing income to the college. Sidewalks began crumbling because of the adobe soil beneath them. Far worse, there were divisions in the school and in the church in Los Angeles. Dissenters started a rival school close to the Hollywood campus before the Bible college even had a chance to move there.

With this dissension, Jackson Deets began to cool in his support of the Hollywood project. Wilson was sympathetic to Deets's point of view but did not want to see an open break between Deets and the school. Wilson and Isaiah Reid, another trustee, were appointed as a committee to find a plan for reorganization that Deets would support. After various suggestions were put forward, Deets dropped his demands except for removing two members from the board that he deemed controversial. One of these resigned, and Deets was satisfied.

In the midst of this, Wilson became pastor of Pasadena First Church and persuaded the other members of the Board of Trustees to sell the Hollywood campus and purchase 134 acres in Pasadena for the development of the school. In January 1910 the trustees voted to buy the Hugus Ranch in Pasadena. Wilson seconded the motion to reserve 50 acres for the school and sell 80 acres to finance the campus. With 50 acres, the school would always have adequate land for expansion. (However, later leaders, in desperate need to erase the school's debt, sold 40 or 50 acres for a low sum—none of which was actually used to liquidate the debt!)

There were expenses—streets to lay out, curbs and sidewalks to put in, and water and electrical services that had to be extended. The Pacific Electric Company also asked a large sum to extend its streetcars out the extra half mile to the campus. Wilson was not pleased with some of the decisions that were made, and he developed a low opinion of the business acumen of some of his colleagues in the ministry.

Wilson was occupied with college business until the end of his life. Jackson Deets and others gave generously to an endowment fund for the college, but the school had problems in its educational and religious programs that aggravated the burden of the financial undertaking. Wilson's involvement with these issues was intimate. He served the college as a trustee, including a term as vice-chairman and later, in the brief interval between Bresee's death and his own, as chairman of the board. In addition, he taught courses at the college while pastoring Pasadena First Church. For Wilson, the problems of starting the college were a constant and heavy burden that was never alleviated.

After nearly three years of pastoring Pasadena First

Church, Wilson resigned and returned to full-time revivalism. District Superintendent John W. Goodwin placed a notice in the *Nazarene Messenger* recommending Wilson as an evangelist, but Goodwin's notice also stated that churches should not try to call Wilson as their pastor, noting that he would have stayed at Pasadena First if pastoral work were his immediate calling. Wilson moved his family back to the orange ranch in Upland and then went to hold his first camp meeting at Milton, California, where Guy had conducted a meeting a few months earlier.

Then fate intervened. The district assembly met, and John Goodwin resigned the superintendency in order to become finance manager for the college in Pasadena. Goodwin's superintendency had not been an easy one—he was stretched, giving much of his time to assisting Los Angeles First Church overcome problems caused by the dissension there, while acting simultaneously as business manager of the college. The college's situation was so dire that Goodwin believed it deserved his full attention. In the aftermath of Goodwin's resignation, the assembly elected W. C. Wilson as its superintendent.

And so in the winter of 1911 the orange ranch was sold, and the Wilsons moved back to Pasadena. A new house was constructed on an acre lot two blocks north of the college, and the family moved into it the following summer.

Wilson's first year as superintendent of the Southern California District was busy. In January 1912, the first Sunday School convention of the Los Angeles and San Francisco districts was held at Los Angeles First Church, lasting two days. But the month was also marked by personal tragedy for Wilson when his beloved daughter Hallie died of septicemia. In spite of his deep grief, the work of the district still had to be done. In March Wilson helped Dr. Bresee organize University Church of the Nazarene in Pasadena and presided over the meeting at which Seth C. Rees was called as pastor.

In April the *Nazarene Messenger,* published in Los Angeles, merged with the *Pentecostal Advocate,* published in Greenville,

Texas, to form the *Herald of Holiness*. To accomplish this, the Nazarene Publishing Company in Los Angeles and the Advocate Publishing Company in Greenville had to merge, and the publishing interests were all relocated to the central location of Kansas City.

An early issue of the *Herald of Holiness* carried a picture of the formal inauguration of Edgar P. Ellyson as president of the Pasadena school. Ellyson had been a general superintendent of the denomination from 1908 to 1911 but declined renomination and election. Wilson participated in the inaugural event and participated as well in the commencement in which college degrees were awarded to three graduates.

For several months during this period, Wilson kept a daily diary—his answer, perhaps, to the pressures of a growing district and the anguish of Hallie's death. Most of the entries concern the details of district supervision. He held revival meetings for home mission churches of the district, checked the legality of church deeds, settled disputes between individuals and churches, and sought funds for district needs and special causes—such as the college, publishing house, and missionary interests. All these and other duties were part of the unceasing work of the district superintendency. Some notations in his diary show the nature of his activity:

"Arranged to hold tent meeting. Looked for a good location."

"To San Bernardino. Preached three times. Attendance 11-15-35. Two halfhearted seekers."

"Bought tent in Los Angeles. Shipped to Santa Ana."

"To L.A. to see Dr. Bresee to talk over sending Athans to El Paso to take charge of our mission work there."

"United two missions at Florence."

"Organized a church at Santa Ana."

About Lura Horton, a minister from the East, he noted: "She preaches well."

Some of his notes were quite candid: "A little meeting in a big tent."

Wilson increasingly sought advice from Bresee on difficult problems that were, he wrote, "too dark and deep for me." Bresee's wisdom was always appreciated.

Wilson had to travel incessantly, but he had no automobile until the final months of his superintendency—and he used it sparingly then. Most often he traveled by train, except in the Los Angeles area, where the Pacific Electric and Los Angeles Railway operated an electric car system. It took from one to three hours to travel from a point in Los Angeles to the corner of the Pasadena College campus, and then there was a half-mile walk up a slight grade to home. In spite of the need to travel, Wilson tried to reach home every night and was never away for more than two or three days at a time.

During a terrific flood that struck the area, the usual streetcars were all stopped. Wilson finally managed to make his way to the bank of the Arroyo Seco. He was on the opposite side from Pasadena, but an old railroad trestle was nearby, and he crossed the raging torrent by way of the span shortly after midnight. About two o'clock, the whole trestle gave way and was swept down the Los Angeles River.

As district superintendent, Wilson was responsible for the religious services and general arrangements of the district camp meeting—a major annual event in the life of Southern California Nazarenes. Although camp meetings were always part of the district culture, the event gained new significance from the time it was first held in the eucalyptus grove that covered several acres of the college campus in Pasadena. The campground and program were admired by every evangelist and by all others who attended the meetings.

While eucalyptus trees do not provide dense shade, the trees were planted in rows, and the tent area and walks were covered with fresh sawdust each year. So, too, were the floors of the white tents, which were arranged in long rows running north and south. Those who did not wish to cook could buy food at a special cafeteria tent that had screened walls to keep out flies. Cots could be rented by those who did not bring their own. Single men could rent cots in the men's quarters of an old building. Other quarters on campus could be rented by single women. Vespers were held on the paths at several places each evening, and then electric lights were turned on.

Around 2,000 or more attended the preaching services, and most of them lived on the grounds for the 10 days of camp. There were typically scenes of great emotion expressed in the preaching services, testimony times, and altar calls. Strangers with little background or understanding of this type of religious expression sometimes wandered in, and some responded to the altar calls.

The annual camp meeting usually featured two prominent evangelists, special singers, and a choir of around 150 members. C. E. Cornell usually was called upon for two things at which he excelled—conducting the altar calls and raising the several thousand dollars to cover the deficit expenses that remained by the final Sunday morning. The deficit was an increasing burden, and the beautiful camp meeting was suspended the year following Wilson's resignation from the district superintendency.

The Pasadena camp included many features in its early days that would later be opposed or deplored. One major service was given to the theme of prohibition. All-night prayer meetings and long altar services were not encouraged. C. E. Cornell would often urge people to get a good night's sleep in order to be fit for the next day's services. The numbers of those converted, restored, or entirely sanctified at these meetings were quite modest, compared to the numbers reported in later years. One year, when nearly 2,000 people were attending the final service, those who had received definite help at the altar were asked to raise their hands. Young Mallalieu Wilson proudly recorded in his diary that a grand total of 20 hands were raised.

14

COLLEAGUES

W. C. Wilson resigned from the superintendency at the annual assembly of the Southern California District in 1915. His precise reasons are unclear, but he made remarks about the stress generated by the detailed work of the office and noted that he had held the position for four years. Financial pressures on the camp meeting, the university, and the district in general were increasing. With the outbreak of World War I in Europe, the Eastern states were beginning to prosper from the production of war materials for the Allied nations, but California was economically depressed, and it remained so even after the United States entered the conflict.

Several of Wilson's friends were confident that he would be elected general superintendent by the Fourth General Assembly meeting in October. This confidence was based partly in the fact that General Superintendents P. F. Bresee and E. F. Walker were both too ill to preside at district assemblies scheduled the previous fall and winter. H. F. Reynolds, the only other general superintendent, was specifically responsible for supervising foreign fields and abbreviated his trip around the world to help fill in for his ailing colleagues. Bresee also asked Wilson to divide his slate with him. Wilson agreed and spent several weeks in the fall of 1914 presiding over district assemblies in the South.

In spite of the expectation that Wilson would be elected to a general office in October, the church at Upland wanted him as their pastor again, even if only for a few months. Wilson accepted their call and considered it "the nearest thing to a real vacation that I ever have had in my life." He was surprised, too, that this short pastorate showed more signs of success than his previous pastorates there and attributed this to the fact that he had "learned a few things since I was here the first time."

Improvements were made to the church building. For instance, their broken-down organ was replaced with a new piano. Also, the congregation contributed to the collection and donation of books to the Pasadena College library. The project was initiated by Dean Paul J. White, and the college library's holdings doubled that summer. The several hundred volumes given by the Upland congregation were stored at the Wilson house, so Mallalieu enjoyed the opportunity for diverse reading before his father transported the books to Pasadena in his Ford.

Wilson purchased his first automobile in the fall of 1914, and the family enjoyed a few trips in it. However, driving made him nervous—whether it was he or his son behind the wheel.

Although there was little time for it, his one recreation at Upland was hunting. Rabbits were about the only wild game available, so when opportunities arose, the family counted on fried rabbit for supper.

Wilson's closest friends in these later years included pastors, teachers, and laymen. The most colorful of these associates was Seth C. Rees, pastor of University Church in Pasadena. Rees and Wilson had many experiences in common, and when Rees moved to California and settled in Pasadena, the two men quickly formed a friendship.

C. E. Cornell, whom Wilson knew before moving to California, was a strong pastor on the district and was a successor to Dr. Bresee as pastor of Los Angeles First Church. Cornell had begun his ministry as a layworker in the YMCA before becoming a minister.

Another close friend was John W. Goodwin. Goodwin and

Wilson were remarkably alike. They were close in age, had arrived in California at about the same time, and had filled many of the same positions. But also there were sharp contrasts in their special abilities and attitudes toward certain church questions. While Wilson was intensely practical and specific, Goodwin was unconcerned with details. His favorite expression was "in general." Bresee's vision, spirit, and ideals for the Church of the Nazarene were exerted after his death through his influence upon John W. Goodwin, who was a general superintendent from 1916 until 1940.

A. O. Hendricks was another friend. An intense person, he served Southern California as pastor, evangelist, and Pasadena College president. He became involved in everything, even when his personal interests might have been improved by staying aloof from the fray. He and Wilson were in fundamental agreement on church matters, and Wilson profoundly respected Hendricks's judgment.

In the last two years of Wilson's life, he developed a very close friendship with a college teacher, Andrew J. Ramsay. On the surface it seemed the two men had little in common. Ramsay had attended a Southern Baptist seminary and pastored Baptist congregations before being filled with the Holy Spirit. He operated a Missionary Baptist school at Diamond Springs, Virginia, until moving to Pasadena in 1913 to teach theology at the Nazarene college.

Ramsay displayed democratic honesty and unpretentiousness. He detested "stuffed shirts." These traits endeared him to Wilson. Ramsay was polished and courteous, with a keen sense of humor and a fund of stories to illustrate his serious points. In his spare time he counseled students and offered positive advice and prayer. Professor Ramsay lived about three blocks from the Wilsons and was a frequent guest. When either Wilson or Ramsay missed a hat or umbrella, he always knew where to find it—he had left it at the other one's home.

Howard Eckel was another Wilson associate. He was a

strong and solid churchman. When Wilson left the superintendency of the Southern California District, he favored Eckel's election as his successor. Wilson was highly amused, however, at Eckel's acceptance speech, for Eckel said to the assembly, "Bring any problems you may have to me. My shoulders are broad." Wilson's response: "He'll feel different about it after a year in the job!"

But Wilson's great leader and friend was Dr. P. F. Bresee. Bresee was the strong patriarchal presence in the Church of the Nazarene along the West Coast. To Wilson he was part father and part prophet. Before Bresee's death, he and Wilson worked together on one last major project: an attempt to avoid what historian Timothy L. Smith called the "Rees dissension."

Bresee and Wilson anticipated possible tragedy resulting from a clash among district leaders and tried to avert it. Even had they lived, they might have been unsuccessful. The crisis began while Wilson was district superintendent and broke over the whole church like a tidal wave a little more than a year after Bresee and Wilson passed from the scene. Seth Rees became a major figure in the conflict, though Wilson and other close friends also were involved. Eckel, who pledged to handle any problem on the district, felt the full force of the conflict, and he and Rees ultimately symbolized antagonistic principles in the history of the early denomination: Rees the desire for freedom, Eckel the search for order.

Wilson early befriended Rees upon his move to California, and as pastor of Pasadena First Church of the Nazarene, he received Rees into membership from the Society of Friends (Quakers). Later, when the University Church of the Nazarene was organized on the campus of the Pasadena College, Wilson, then district superintendent, persuaded the church to call Rees as its pastor. The peaceful beginning was followed by ripples of trouble, and then by a more serious situation involving an ordained elder and his disciplinary mistreatment of his two teenage sons. Rees sought to oust the elder from the church immediately, but summer supply pastor A. J. Ramsay wanted to secure the decision in proper fashion by following the prescribed *Manual* procedure. Forceful personalities were involved, and mutual adjustment and cooperation were necessary to avert an impasse, but these were in short supply. Wilson's involvement in the issue drove a wedge in his relationship with Rees that was not removed until a few hours before Wilson's death.

Another clash further alienated the two old friends. Before district assembly, Wilson prepared a list of prospective committee members, taking the journal of the previous assembly and revising the lists as he thought appropriate. Bresee presided at the assembly and reached the point during which he asked the delegates the standard question, "How will you raise the assembly committees?" Someone moved that they be appointed by the chair. With no objection or discussion, the motion carried. Bresee then reached into his pocket, pulled out the list Wilson had prepared, and read it.

Although this occurred in good Methodist fashion, Rees took the floor and expressed his dissatisfaction with this method of conducting church business. Wilson, both amused and irritated, was obliged to respond with an equally pointed speech. Holiness preachers of that day were seemingly accustomed to blunt attacks and often confronted opposition within the mainline denominations. Responses were not always couched in diplomatic language. Though Rees personally attacked Bresee in the *Herald of Holiness,* neither Bresee nor Wilson considered expelling Rees from the denomination. They agreed, however, that he should leave his pastorate at University Church, though they knew this was unlikely. The previous year, Rees had rejected the invitation to pastor a good church 100 miles from Pasadena.

The breach between Wilson and Rees greatly distressed Sarah Wilson. The afternoon before her husband's death she became so burdened over the unreconciled relationship that she dropped to her knees and prayed for God to send Rees to their home. Shortly afterward, she heard a noise at the front of the house and went to the door, where she saw Rees hurriedly exiting the front gate. He had left a check for $25 under the porch door and insisted he could not come inside just then. Sarah brushed aside his protests and brought him in, where he had a brief talk and prayer with the dying Wilson. There were no profuse apologies or emotional expressions, but those who knew both men realized that this was a real restoration of fellowship. Wilson's last words indicated this, and Rees's prayer at the funeral could have been given only by one who was reconciled.

15

THE HIGHEST OFFICE

Wilson greeted the approaching Fourth General Assembly with a mixture of emotions. Friends assured him that he would be elected general superintendent. He did not entirely welcome the prospect. For one thing, the office did not carry a respectable salary. In 1915 the church did not have a general budget out of which to pay its officers, and the meager offerings divided among the church's general superintendents did not even give each one an income equal to that of a preacher with a small pastorate. Bresee lived with one of his sons, who largely supported him. E. F. Walker procured income from Olivet University. H. F. Reynolds was also the church's general missionary secretary and obtained his income from that office, not from the general superintendency.

Wilson had tasted the sacrifice himself. The district assemblies he had conducted for Bresee and Walker in 1914 had been with the smallest and poorest districts in the South. Wilson had received little more than his bare traveling expenses, if that, and upon returning home he had gone to the bank to borrow a few hundred dollars. For the first time in all his years in California, he was turned down.

Partly for these reasons, and perhaps partly for others, Wilson told his son that he even believed the church could abolish the office of general superintendent after Bresee's death. Other leaders expressed similar views at the time. This was not Bresee's own view, however, nor that of Reynolds. The two senior general superintendents had no illusions about the necessity of their work. They knew that many district superintendents were not able to settle all the problems on their districts and that some district superintendents were themselves problems that needed a superior officer to manage. Wilson would serve in the highest office if elected, but he had no illusions about it.

Two factors complicated the election of general superintendents in 1915: the number who should be elected and their geographic distribution. Two of the three incumbents—Bresee and Walker—were from the Southern California District. Wilson, who was a strong contender for the office, was from the same district. General Superintendent H. F. Reynolds lived in Kansas City and was a member of the Kansas District. To balance regional sensitivities, Reynolds had also lived in Brooklyn, Chicago, and Oklahoma City since his first election in 1907.

The General Assembly met from September 30 to October 11 in Kansas City. On the eighth day, the three incumbent general superintendents were reelected without the regional issue being raised. Wilson placed fourth, just behind the incumbents, with 92 of the 147 votes needed to elect and 40 votes ahead of E. P. Ellyson, who was in fifth place.

Once the assembly decided to elect a fourth general superintendent, however, the place of residence became a live issue. The issue of a fourth general superintendent was raised by Dr. Bresee, whose health was failing so rapidly that he was being kept alive only by the constant medical attention of his son, a physician. Bresee hoped only for enough energy to finish the assembly and return home to die in peace. Dr. Walker had also been too ill recently to carry the full share of his duties. Bresee bluntly told the assembly that it had only one "real" general superintendent—Dr. Reynolds. Walker was furious at the remark and protested that he too was a general superintendent. Bresee was too near the end to argue the question or avoid the direct challenge. He said: "I repeat: you have only one general superintendent and should elect another."

The whole matter of electing a fourth superintendent was further exacerbated by rising sectional feeling inflamed by an intemperate remark by C. E. Cornell. The pastor of Los Angeles First Church was usually tactful in all he said, but in opposing large assembly committees, he said: "There are a lot of the brethren from places like Texas who are as good as they can be but are as ignorant of parliamentary law as Hottentots." The remark was contrary to all rules of parliamentary discussion and also false: the favorite study of Texans was public speaking and debate, and Robert's *Rules of Order* was next to the Bible and the *Manual* in their devotion. Seth Rees jumped to his feet and demanded Cornell's apology. Cornell did just that, hastily and profusely, but the resentment stirred in the Southern delegates by that remark flared up in a new determination to oppose the election of any new leaders from southern California and an unwillingness to endorse measures proposed by delegates from that region.

The most immediate effect was a campaign that was begun to elect E. P. Ellyson, who had served in the office from 1908 to 1911. Delegates began receiving messages saying "Elect Ellyson." Even Wilson's daughter, Bertha, received such a message. After several ballots were taken, Wilson withdrew his name from further consideration. He had never before fought for an office in the church, and the tensions surrounding this issue were beginning to overwhelm him. That night in his hotel room he suffered what was probably a heart attack, or at least a serious nervous attack. Bertha and Haldor Lillenas stayed with him through the night, and Bertha later told the rest of the family that her father's legs were as cold as ice.

With Wilson's withdrawal, Ellyson was elected on the 10th ballot. Ellyson was not in attendance but arrived three days after his election. To the immense surprise of delegates, he declined. Unknown to most, Ellyson was the silent victim of a false but vicious rumor of the sort that is hopeless to fight. His greatness was shown by the way he refused to let it embitter his sweet spirit or turn him from such fields of usefulness as he could find in the church. In 1923 the Sixth General Assembly sent him to Kansas City to be founder of the denomination's Department of Church Schools, which he headed with distinction for two decades.

Ellyson's refusal to accept his election paved the road for Wilson's election as general superintendent. After a General Assembly of ups and downs, it happened on the morning of Monday, October 11. His election on the 11th ballot was declared by Dr. Walker, who chaired the session. According to the official minutes of the assembly, "Dr. Bresee presented and introduced Brother Wilson as the fourth General Superintendent.* After Brother Wilson made a few remarks, Dr. Bresee led in a short prayer for the blessing of the Lord upon the new General Superintendent. The Assembly broke into the song 'Blest Be the Tie That Binds' and 'I Love Thy Church, O God.'"

Wilson's election meant that three of four general superintendents were from southern California, and he discussed with Bresee the likelihood of moving to the Southeast in order to keep peace in the church. Wilson was quite willing to do so, especially if he could locate in Nashville, near his Kentucky home country and the area where he had evangelized for many years. Bresee advised him against this course, since his own imminent death would soon change the equation.

Wilson's superintendency began even before he left the General Assembly site in Kansas City. He was assigned assemblies in Texas and Oklahoma, so he went to the Pentecostal Nazarene Publishing House to arrange the transfer of report blanks to pastors and others on the districts. A number of details later assigned to the district secretary were cared for by the general superintendents in those early years. Some districts already wanted to change their assembly dates. Some district

---

*Wilson was the fifth general superintendent in the denomination's history, but the fourth elected in this particular assembly.

superintendents wanted advice about what to do with ministers out of good standing who wanted to return. Some district secretaries had problems about procedures that had never been clearly detailed in the *Manual*. Wilson did not type, so his answers to these problems were dictated to a secretary.

After arranging for the round of assemblies in November, Wilson returned to California. He greeted his wife with the words "Well, Miss Sarah, your husband went off a plain elder and returned a bishop."

"Yes," was her rejoinder, "and you went off with a job with regular pay each week and came back with nothing!"

Wilson told his son they would move to the South as soon as he returned from district assemblies scheduled over the next two months, and he went to visit Dr. Bresee, who was very weak but clear-minded in his final days.

Letters came every few days from Dr. Reynolds about missionary applicants, the *Manual,* and countless other details. On some matters Wilson went to nearby Glendora to consult Dr. Walker. In a letter to prominent Nashville layman John T. Benson, Wilson also indicated that he might delay his proposed move to that city—the move would be expensive, and property values in California were depressed. He confided to Mallalieu that he also thought it best to wait until fall and thus avoid the hot weather.

Wilson began his round of assemblies in early November. He enjoyed the work and experienced the same cordial spirit he had encountered in the Southern assemblies the previous year. The Dallas District Assembly was conducted first, opening on November 3. The assembly passed a resolution requesting that "as our Jr. Gen. Supt. is to make his residence in the South, that he look carefully over the Dallas District in selecting a place of residence." He went next to the Hamlin (now West Texas) District Assembly, again presiding over the legislative sessions. Here he was reunited with his old friend from Kentucky, Methodist preacher Henry Clay Morrison, one of the patriarchs of the Southern Holiness Movement. Wilson and Morrison, together with two of the ministers from the district, preached in the evenings. The preaching was anointed, and there were many seekers. After convening the evening session of November 13, Wilson read to the assembly a telegram announcing the sad news that his confidant and colleague Dr. Bresee had died earlier in the day.

Wilson went next to conduct the San Antonio District Assembly. By this time he was complaining to associates of a lack of sleep. He also was unable to find food that agreed with him. His condition worsened, and he did no more than open the assembly in San Antonio when he announced that he would be asking District Superintendent William E. Fisher to preside in his stead. The report in the *Herald of Holiness* stated that "his parting words to us were 'Keep the glory down; push the battle for holiness,' after which he quietly left the Assembly room, having suffered intensely the night before with appendicitis." Wilson took a train straight for California.

Once home, Wilson's physician disagreed with his self-diagnosis and stated that the condition was a combination of digestive and liver trouble. Wilson was ordered to bed for several weeks and urged not to work for at least a month. He was also referred to a specialist in Los Angeles to remove an impacted wisdom tooth that was ulcerated. The tooth had to be sawed out.

After the cruelly painful operation, Wilson somehow suffered the long ride back to Pasadena on the interurban car and the lengthy walk to his house from the local car. He was in agony and suffered an entire week before his physician returned with other specialists. The wound in his jaw was treated, which gave some relief, but he continued suffering in bed and finally woke up one night with excruciating pains in his head. The doctor did not seem concerned about the seriousness of the condition, but from that point on the pain never eased.

Sarah was very uneasy with her husband's condition. Pastor A. O. Hendricks, in the midst of his usual rush, stopped his car to ask Mallalieu about his father.

"He's doing nicely, I suppose?"

"The doctor says he is all right, but Mother and I have the feeling that he is never going to get well."

Hendricks instantly drove to the Wilson home, where he summoned a lawyer and a doctor. The lawyer drew up a deed that would give Sarah ownership of the house—the only asset that W. C. Wilson possessed. Soon an ambulance arrived, and the doctor explained that Wilson would be taken to a hospital for observation. "It's nothing serious. He'll be back in a few days," he assured the family.

Wilson was conscious but could not speak. The family feared that his condition was more serious than the doctor realized or would admit. Wilson felt that way also. Later, in the hospital, he told Sarah: "Tell Brother Hendricks and Brother Cornell," followed by a pause, "and all my brethren that Jesus never disappointed me and that He did not fail me in my last moments. Yes, I am going away, forever to be with the Lord. But there's not a fear, not a cloud, but all is clear." In the early morning hours of December 19, 1915, Wilson passed away.

All day Sunday the family phone was busy with news reporters seeking information. The funeral was set for Thursday afternoon so that Guy, away holding a revival in the blizzard-bound Dakotas, could reach Los Angeles in time to attend. But the *Los Angeles Times* printed the funeral day as Tuesday, and hundreds of people inadvertently came from all over southern California on that day. The paper published a correction, but when Guy sent late word that his train could not get him home until Friday it was too late to publish a second correction. The funeral was held on Thursday, as originally scheduled, with interment delayed until Friday so that Guy could be present.

The funeral was at Los Angeles First Church. Wilson's

body lay in state at the same spot where Dr. Bresee's casket had stood less than five weeks before. Once again the entire faculty and student body of Nazarene University gathered with hundreds of ministers and laity to pay their respects to a church leader. Messages were read from H. F. Reynolds and others, but the speakers were all Wilson's close personal friends from the Southern California District.

C. E. Cornell presided and spoke of his association with Wilson in the pre-California days, when both were Methodist evangelists. John W. Goodwin read scriptures and spoke of their mutual concerns. District Superintendent Howard Eckel spoke briefly. Seth Rees led in prayer. A. O. Hendricks preached the sermon at Wilson's prior request. H. Orton Wiley closed in prayer, while Wilson's closest friend, Prof. A. J. Ramsay, pronounced the benediction.

By the following day Guy had arrived, and W. C. Wilson was laid to rest in the beautiful Mountain View Cemetery in Pasadena next to his daughter, Hallie Franklin.

The news of Wilson's death stunned the whole denomination. Bresee's death was long anticipated, and Wilson, at age 49, had been elected to the general superintendency precisely to fill that expected vacancy. Now he too was gone to be with the Lord! Many people wondered how this could happen when Wilson seemed to possess the right combination of wisdom and vigor for the general superintendency of a united denomination not even a decade old. In less than 40 days the church had gone from four general superintendents to two, and only one of these—H. F. Reynolds—was in good health. Two men were elected by the district superintendents to succeed Bresee and Wilson: John W. Goodwin of California and Roy T. Williams of Texas. The workmen were buried, but the work went on.

Sarah Wilson continued living in the house in Pasadena for the rest of her life, teaching for several years in the academy division (high school) of Nazarene University. The influence of her husband lived on, however, in the college, the district, and the lives of their children and grandchildren.

From the day in 1903 when W. C. Wilson united with Los Angeles First Church, the Wilson family has given an unbroken line of clergy to the Church of the Nazarene. Bertha Wilson Lillenas was one who carried on her father's legacy. Her sermon "Christian Freedom" was included in a collection of notable sermons published in the 1920s under the title *The Nazarene Pulpit*. Mallalieu was also ordained to the Nazarene ministry and combined college teaching with periods of pastoral ministry. Guy returned to the Methodist Church of his youth but was conscious of his father's lasting influence upon his ministry. And that impulse has continued into each subsequent generation of W. C. Wilson's descendants, from preacher-grandsons M. Archie Wilson Jr., Donald Grobe, and Elwyn Grobe, to great-grandson Larry Wilson's ordination in 1991 on the New England District, which marked the fourth generation of W. C. Wilson's family to serve the universal Church of God and the Church of the Nazarene through the ordained ministry.